VICTORIA & ALBERT MUSEUM
DIARY 2004

FRANCES LINCOLN

Frances Lincoln Limited
4 Torriano Mews
Torriano Avenue
London NW5 2RZ
www.franceslincoln.com

The V&A Diary 2004
Copyright © Frances Lincoln Limited 2003
Text and photographs copyright
© Victoria and Albert Museum, London
Licensed by V&A Enterprises Limited

Every effort has been made to seek permission to reproduce those images whose copyright does not reside with the V&A. Any omissions are entirely unintentional and the details should be addressed to V&A Enterprises Limited, 160 Brompton Road, London SW3 1HW.

Astronomical information reproduced, with permission, from data supplied by HM Nautical Almanac Office, copyright © Council for the Central Laboratory of the Research Councils.

All rights reserved. No part of this publication may be reproduced, stored in a retrieval system or transmitted, in any form, or by any means, electronic, mechanical, photocopying, recording or otherwise, without either prior permission in writing from the publishers or a licence permitting restricted copying. In the United Kingdom such licences are issued by the Copyright Licensing Agency, 90 Tottenham Court Road, London W1P 9HE.

British Library cataloguing-in-publication data
A catalogue record for this book is available from the British Library

ISBN 0-7112-2175-8

Printed in China

First Frances Lincoln edition 2003

VISITORS' INFORMATION
The Victoria and Albert Museum
Cromwell Road
South Kensington, London SW7 2RL
Telephone: 020 7942 2000

Museum hours of opening: daily 10 am to 5.45 pm
Closed: Christmas Eve, Christmas Day and Boxing Day
Late View opening until 10 pm: every Wednesday and the last Friday in every month

For information on the V&A Museum, please visit the website on www.vam.ac.uk. For information on V&A inspired products, please visit the V&A Museum shop website on www.vandashop.co.uk.

For information on joining the Friends of the V&A, please contact the Friends Office on 020 7942 2271

COVER: *Page of a textile sample book for the Spanish and Portuguese markets, produced for John Kelly, a Norwich worsted manufacturer. Worsted wool samples mounted on paper. English, 1763.*

calendar 2004

January
M	T	W	T	F	S	S
			1	2	3	4
5	6	7	8	9	10	11
12	13	14	15	16	17	18
19	20	21	22	23	24	25
26	27	28	29	30	31	

February
M	T	W	T	F	S	S
						1
2	3	4	5	6	7	8
9	10	11	12	13	14	15
16	17	18	19	20	21	22
23	24	25	26	27	28	29

March
M	T	W	T	F	S	S
1	2	3	4	5	6	7
8	9	10	11	12	13	14
15	16	17	18	19	20	21
22	23	24	25	26	27	28
29	30	31				

April
M	T	W	T	F	S	S
			1	2	3	4
5	6	7	8	9	10	11
12	13	14	15	16	17	18
19	20	21	22	23	24	25
26	27	28	29	30		

May
M	T	W	T	F	S	S
					1	2
3	4	5	6	7	8	9
10	11	12	13	14	15	16
17	18	19	20	21	22	23
24	25	26	27	28	29	30
31						

June
M	T	W	T	F	S	S
	1	2	3	4	5	6
7	8	9	10	11	12	13
14	15	16	17	18	19	20
21	22	23	24	25	26	27
28	29	30				

July
M	T	W	T	F	S	S
			1	2	3	4
5	6	7	8	9	10	11
12	13	14	15	16	17	18
19	20	21	22	23	24	25
26	27	28	29	30	31	

August
M	T	W	T	F	S	S
						1
2	3	4	5	6	7	8
9	10	11	12	13	14	15
16	17	18	19	20	21	22
23	24	25	26	27	28	29
30	31					

September
M	T	W	T	F	S	S
		1	2	3	4	5
6	7	8	9	10	11	12
13	14	15	16	17	18	19
20	21	22	23	24	25	26
27	28	29	30			

October
M	T	W	T	F	S	S
				1	2	3
4	5	6	7	8	9	10
11	12	13	14	15	16	17
18	19	20	21	22	23	24
25	26	27	28	29	30	31

November
M	T	W	T	F	S	S
1	2	3	4	5	6	7
8	9	10	11	12	13	14
15	16	17	18	19	20	21
22	23	24	25	26	27	28
29	30					

December
M	T	W	T	F	S	S
		1	2	3	4	5
6	7	8	9	10	11	12
13	14	15	16	17	18	19
20	21	22	23	24	25	26
27	28	29	30	31		

calendar 2005

January
M	T	W	T	F	S	S
					1	2
3	4	5	6	7	8	9
10	11	12	13	14	15	16
17	18	19	20	21	22	23
24	25	26	27	28	29	30
31						

February
M	T	W	T	F	S	S
	1	2	3	4	5	6
7	8	9	10	11	12	13
14	15	16	17	18	19	20
21	22	23	24	25	26	27
28						

March
M	T	W	T	F	S	S
	1	2	3	4	5	6
7	8	9	10	11	12	13
14	15	16	17	18	19	20
21	22	23	24	25	26	27
28	29	30	31			

April
M	T	W	T	F	S	S
				1	2	3
4	5	6	7	8	9	10
11	12	13	14	15	16	17
18	19	20	21	22	23	24
25	26	27	28	29	30	

May
M	T	W	T	F	S	S
						1
2	3	4	5	6	7	8
9	10	11	12	13	14	15
16	17	18	19	20	21	22
23	24	25	26	27	28	29
30	31					

June
M	T	W	T	F	S	S
		1	2	3	4	5
6	7	8	9	10	11	12
13	14	15	16	17	18	19
20	21	22	23	24	25	26
27	28	29	30			

July
M	T	W	T	F	S	S
				1	2	3
4	5	6	7	8	9	10
11	12	13	14	15	16	17
18	19	20	21	22	23	24
25	26	27	28	29	30	31

August
M	T	W	T	F	S	S
1	2	3	4	5	6	7
8	9	10	11	12	13	14
15	16	17	18	19	20	21
22	23	24	25	26	27	28
29	30	31				

September
M	T	W	T	F	S	S
			1	2	3	4
5	6	7	8	9	10	11
12	13	14	15	16	17	18
19	20	21	22	23	24	25
26	27	28	29	30		

October
M	T	W	T	F	S	S
					1	2
3	4	5	6	7	8	9
10	11	12	13	14	15	16
17	18	19	20	21	22	23
24	25	26	27	28	29	30
31						

November
M	T	W	T	F	S	S
	1	2	3	4	5	6
7	8	9	10	11	12	13
14	15	16	17	18	19	20
21	22	23	24	25	26	27
28	29	30				

December
M	T	W	T	F	S	S
			1	2	3	4
5	6	7	8	9	10	11
12	13	14	15	16	17	18
19	20	21	22	23	24	25
26	27	28	29	30	31	

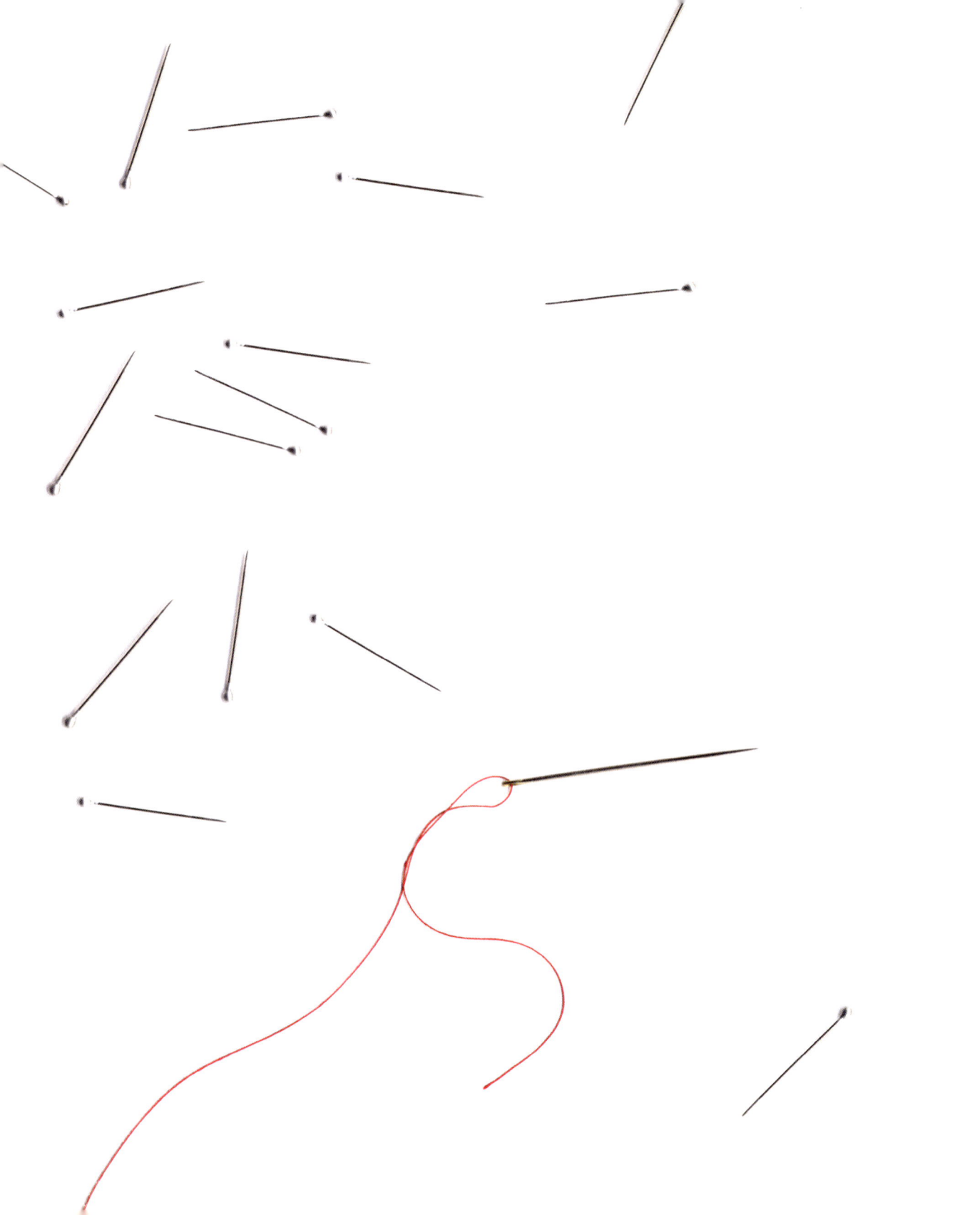

INTRODUCTION

The British Galleries at the V&A display the most comprehensive collection of British design on view anywhere in the world. Among the displays are exceptional examples of textile art and fashion spanning four hundred years, many of them illustrated in this diary.

The wide range of textiles and clothing in the Galleries demonstrates their fundamental place in people's lives and shows how we have always looked beyond the utilitarian – warmth, protection, decency – to bring decoration and colour, as well as style and fashion, to our clothes and surroundings. Textiles are associated with the deeply personal life stages of birth, childhood, marriage and death. Here are outstanding examples of the skill and creativity of individual men and women.

The textiles and clothing illustrated here include examples of weaving, printing and embroidery. The weaving of wool for furnishing and dress fabrics has been a significant manufacturing industry in Britain for many hundreds of years, and in the seventeenth century the silk weaving industry also became established. By the following century the design and quality of British silks, particularly those woven in Spitalfields, was of a high enough standard to rival the silks of the fashion-setting French. They were widely exported, as too were Norwich worsteds, which a contemporary writer described as 'composed of the richest and most brilliant dyes which surpassed any others in Europe'.

Textiles with printed patterns grew increasingly popular for clothing and furnishings from the middle of the eighteenth century. From the sixteenth century to the nineteenth, embroidered textiles played a major part in the comfort and decoration of homes in Britain. This was in large part because they could be made in a domestic setting, and girls learnt needlework as an essential part of their education. Such work is characteristically full of references to the natural world, flowers, animals and other living things. But British taste also relished the exotic, and with the establishment of trade routes with Asia, there grew a market keen for imported textiles in unfamiliar colours and unexpected patterns, to challenge and inspire textile manufacturing in Britain.

Clare Browne Curator, European Textiles 1600–1830

December/January

WEEK 1

29 Monday

30 Tuesday

First Quarter
31 Wednesday

New Year's Eve
1 Thursday

New Year's Day
Holiday UK, Republic of Ireland, Canada, USA, Australia and New Zealand
2 Friday

Holiday, Scotland and New Zealand
3 Saturday

4 Sunday

Martha Edlin's embroidered casket (detail). *Wood covered in panels of satin, embroidered with coloured silks and metal thread. English, 1671.*

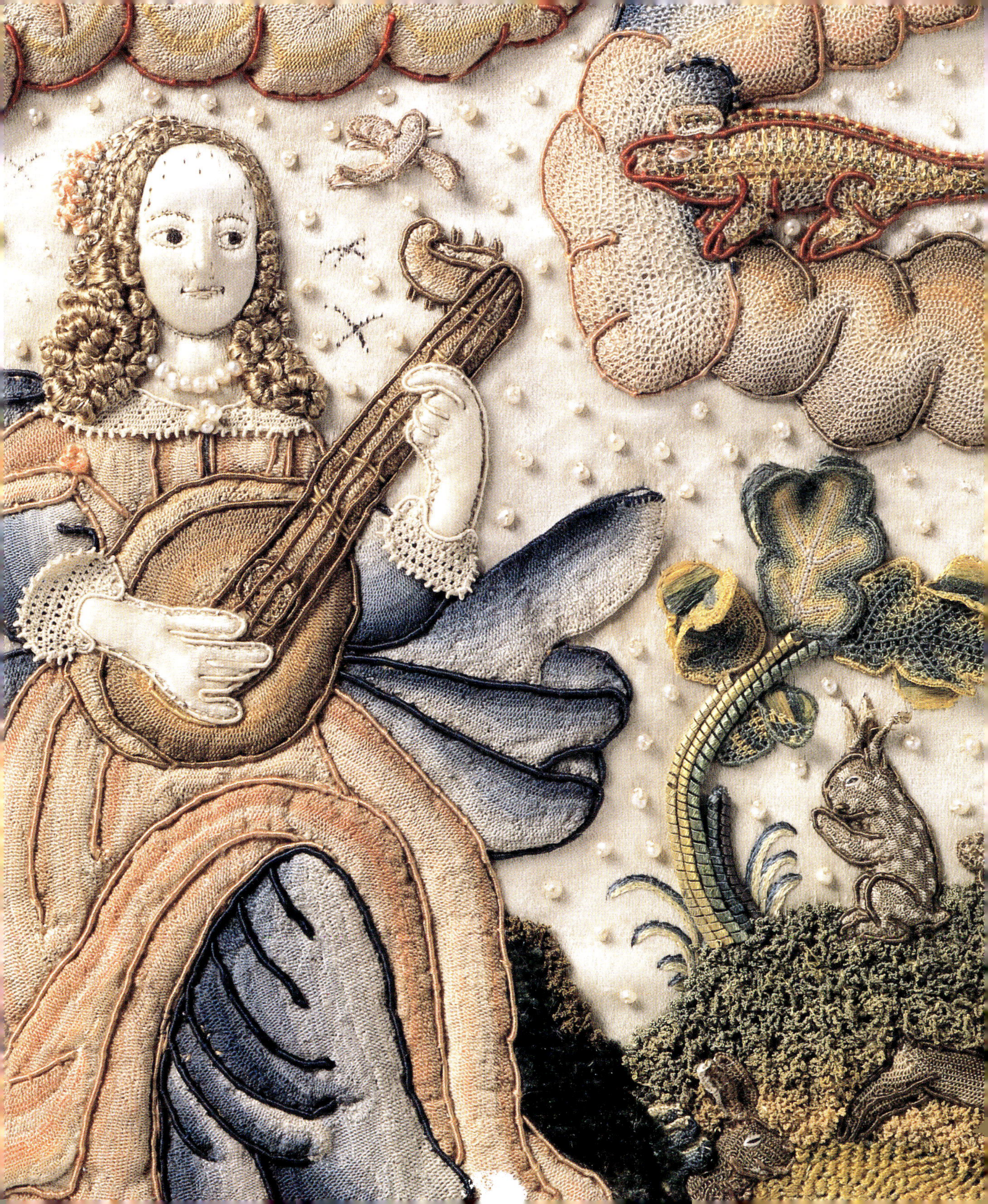

WEEK 2   January

Monday 5

Tuesday 6

Epiphany

Wednesday 7

Full Moon

Hospice flowers 10.30.
Yealman-Legs 2.30.

Thursday 8

Friday 9

Saturday 10

Sunday 11

Silk damask bed curtain, from a bed formerly at Leeds Castle, Kent. Probably woven in Italy or France, or possibly in Spitalfields, London, about 1710.

January

WEEK 3

12 Monday

13 Tuesday

14 Wednesday
Me - Dentist 11.20.

15 Thursday

Last Quarter
16 Friday

17 Saturday

18 Sunday

Samples of aniline-dyed cloth, from The Practical Mechanic's Journal: Record of the Great Exhibition. *English, 1862.*

COAL TAR DYES.

SPECIMENS OF FABRICS DYED WITH
Simpson, Maule & Nicholson's COLORS.

Concentrated Regina Purple.

Concentrated Violet with a little Roseine.

Phosphine.

Roseine.

Regina Purple.

Violet.

Phosphine.

Printers Roseine.

Regina Purple.

No. 2 Violet.

No. 1 Blue.

Blue.

No. 2 Blue & Violet.

Concentrated Printers Roseine.

SPECIMENS OF FABRICS DYED WITH
Perkin & Son's Colors.

SVNBVRY
TVDDINGTON
THORP
SHEPERTON
HAMPTON
HAMPTON·COVRT
CHERSEY
WALTON
WEST
MOVLSAY
OTELANDES
WAYBRIDGE
E·MOVLSAY
DITT
ESHERE
CHESING
HORSEHYLL
BYFLET
WINSLEY
COVEHAM
EB
PIRFORD
STOKE
ASH
NEWARKE
LETHERHEAD
OCKEHAM
FETCHAM
WOKINGE
RIPLEY
BOKEHAM
SEND
EFFINGHAM

WEEK 4   January

Miss Clarke - Solicitor Will 11am.

Monday 19

Holiday, USA (Martin Luther King's birthday)

Tuesday 20

Wilson's to Dinner 4.30.

Wednesday 21

New Moon

Xwoman - 2.30pm Legs V.

Thursday 22

Chinese New Year

John Dentist 10.50.
Rachel Flagg 10am.
Digby Hall. 6pm.

Friday 23

Saturday 24

Sunday 25

Fragment from a large tapestry map, woven in wool and silk at the Sheldon Tapestry workshops. English, about 1588.

January/February

WEEK 5

26 Monday — Massage 11am.

Holiday, Australia (Australia Day)

27 Tuesday — Roger to Cuppa 4.30.

28 Wednesday — Jeev 12.0.

29 Thursday — Chris/Nvie 9am.

First Quarter

30 Friday — Dr Latham 10am.
Hair 1.30.

31 Saturday

1 Sunday

Roller-printed cotton furnishing fabric, printed by Samuel Matley and Son, Hodge, Cheshire. English, 1818.

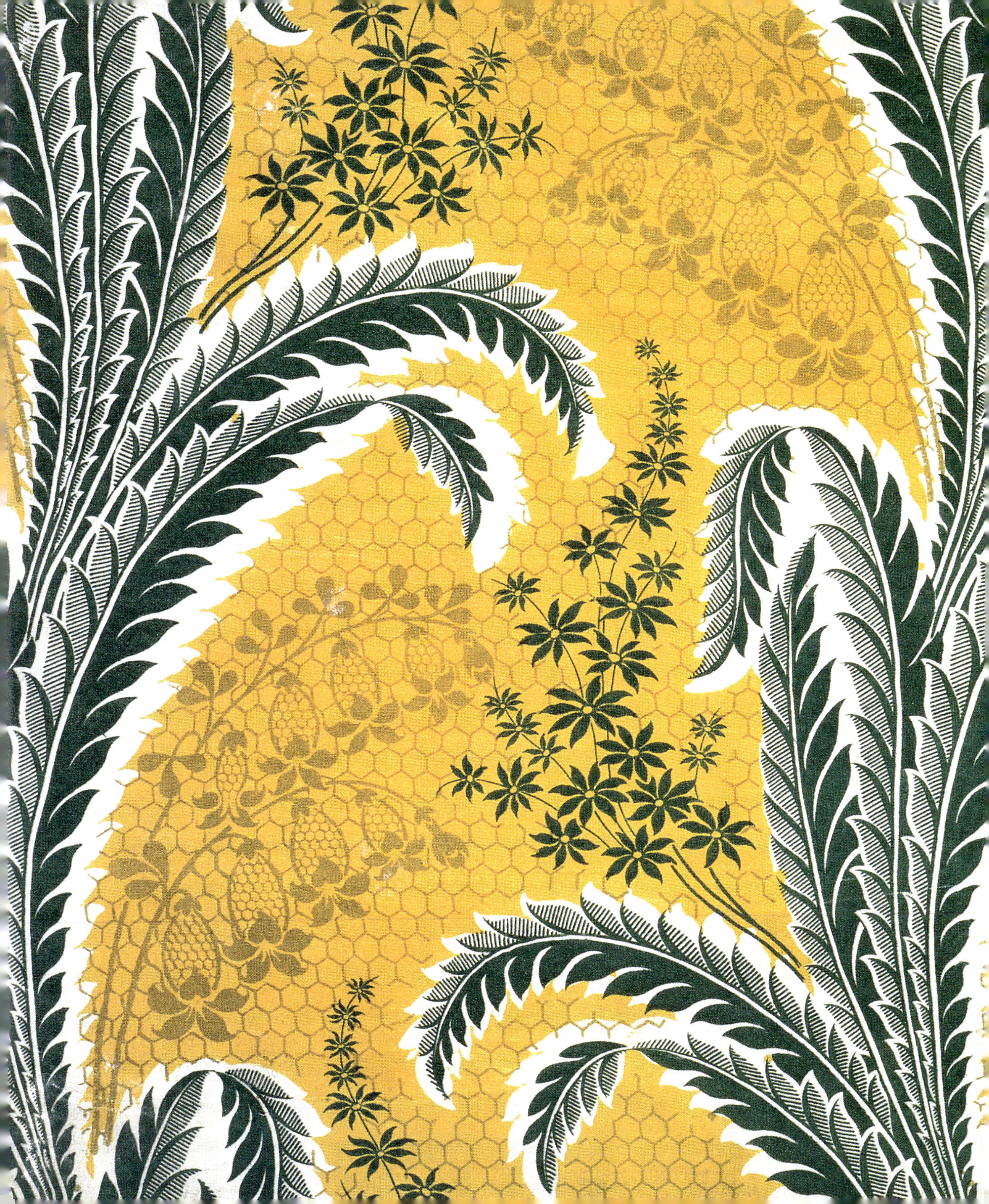

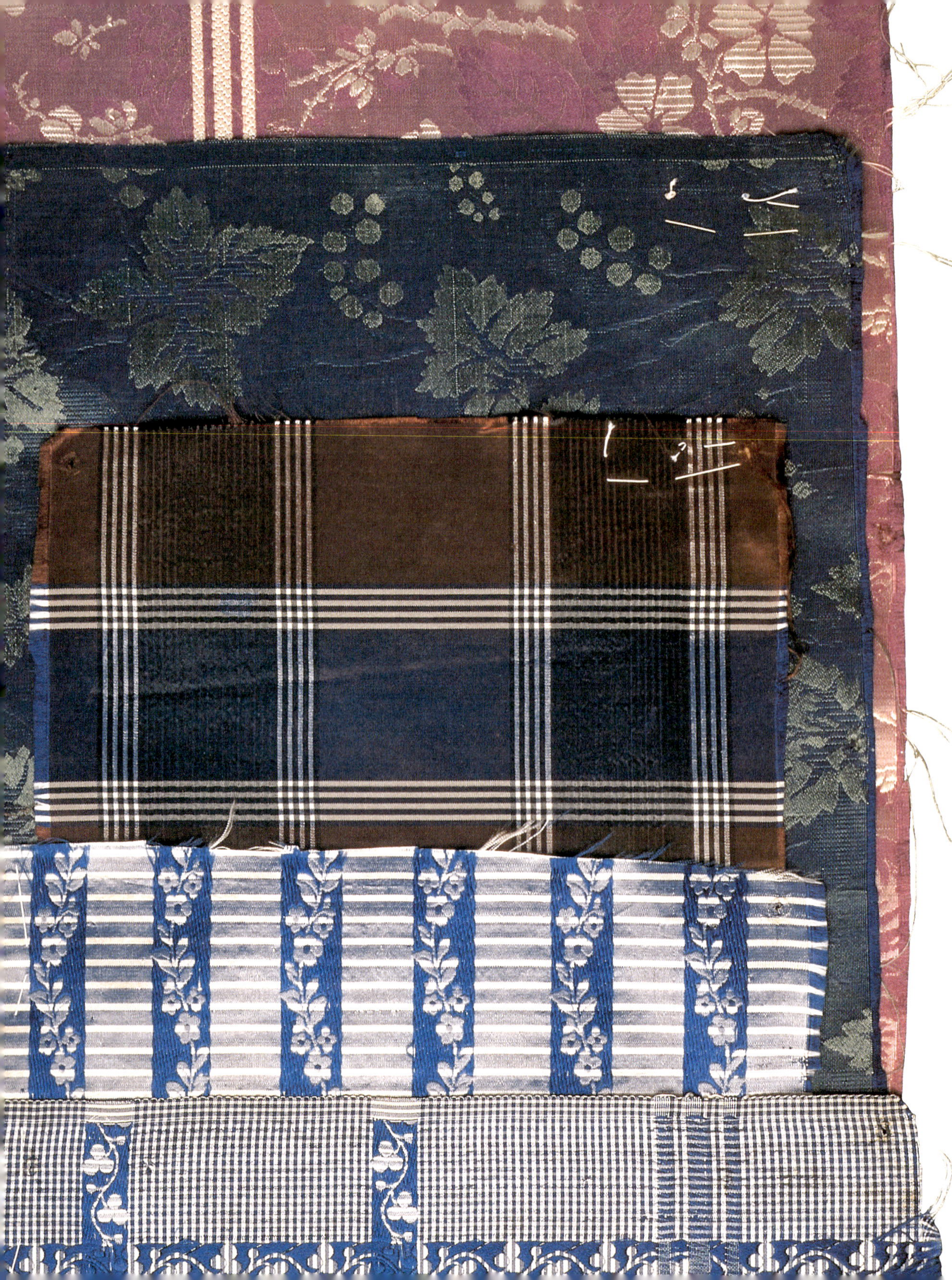

WEEK 6 — February

Monday 2 — Tim - the garden 8.30.

Tuesday 3 — Chrissie 10.30.

Wednesday 4 — June Gabriella Lunch Pub 12.30. Hospice 10.30.

Thursday 5 — Hubbas Tea 4pm. Christine 9am

Friday 6 — Hair 2.45pm.

Full Moon
Holiday, New Zealand (Waitangi Day)

Saturday 7

Sunday 8 — Gabriella to Lunch 12.30.

Woven silk dress fabric textile samples, made by Winkworth and Proctor, Manchester. English, 1850–1851.

February

WEEK 7

9 Monday

10 Tuesday

11 Wednesday

Ham 12.15.

12 Thursday

Christine 9am
Johnnes 'B' - Little Berwick 12.45.

Holiday, USA (Lincoln's birthday)

13 Friday

Montague.

Last Quarter

14 Saturday

St Valentine's Day

15 Sunday

Design for printed cotton by William Kilburn.
English, about 1790.

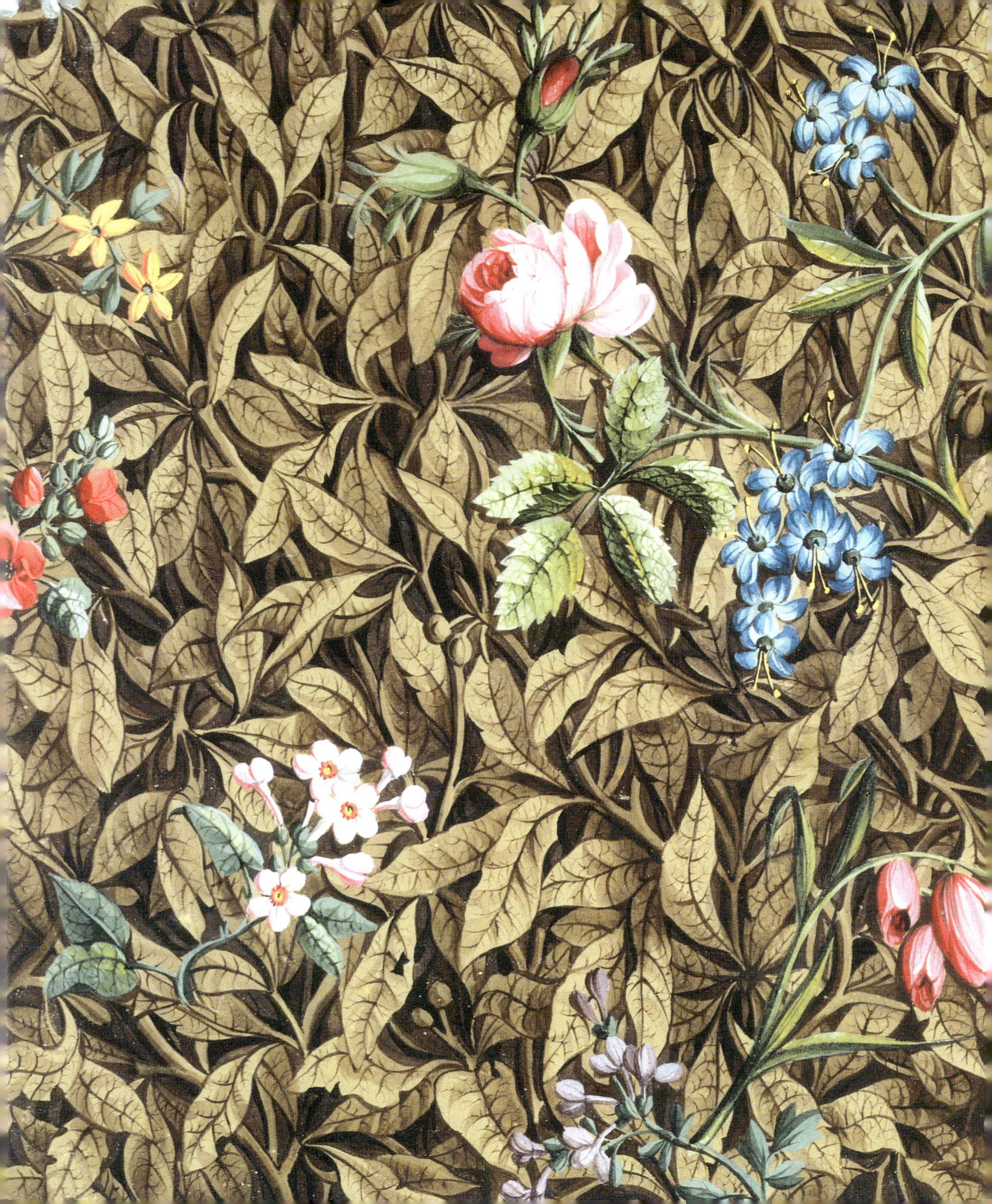

WEEK 8 — February

Monday 16
Holiday, USA (Presidents' Day)

Tuesday 17
Jackie Lunch Little Berwick 12.30.

Wednesday 18
Feet 11.30. Marica Tea 3.30.

Thursday 19
Yeoman 2.30.

Friday 20
Hair 2.15.
New Moon

Saturday 21

Sunday 22
Islamic New Year (subject to sighting of the moon)

Design for a brocaded silk, by Anna Maria Garthwaite for the London weaver Daniel Vautier. Watercolour on paper. English, 1745.

February

WEEK 9

23 Monday

24 Tuesday

Shrove Tuesday
25 Wednesday

Ash Wednesday
26 Thursday

27 Friday

28 Saturday

First Quarter
29 Sunday

Roller-printed, cotton furnishing fabric, probably designed in the studio of Christopher Dresser, London, and printed by the firm of Steiner & Co., Lancashire. English, 1899.

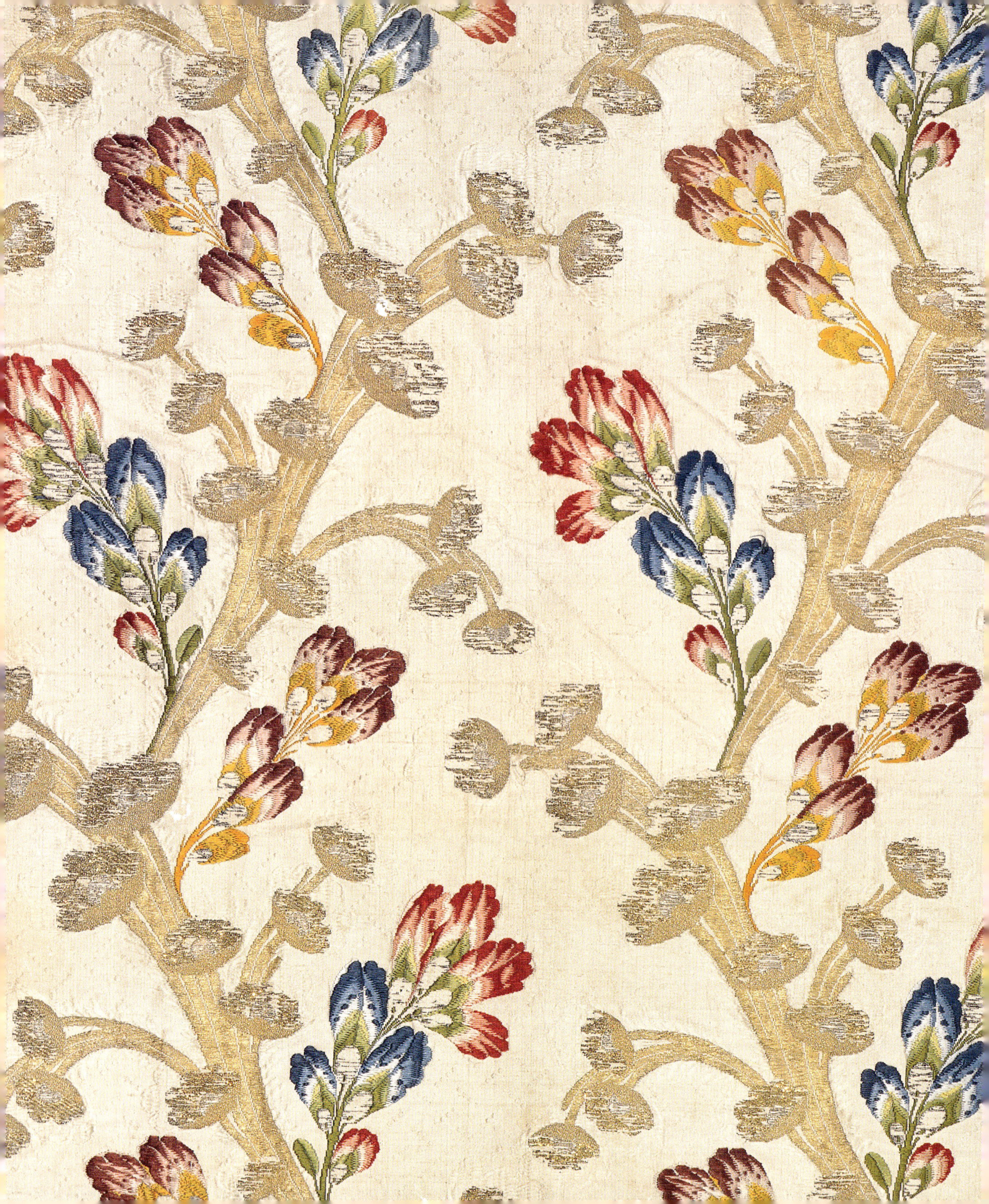

WEEK 10 March

Monday 1 — St David's Day
Tim - Garden £40
Time to Share 4pm.

Tuesday 2
Ruth - Helyar 1pm.

Wednesday 3
Hospice 10.30.
Legs 3.15.

Thursday 4
Yearman. Comprehensive Vocking

Friday 5
Hair 1.30.
Choir Practice 7pm.

Saturday 6

Sunday 7 — Full Moon

Silk brocaded dress fabric with coloured silks and metal thread. Woven in Lyon. French, 1750-1760.

March

WEEK 11

8 Monday

Commonwealth Day

9 Tuesday

10 Wednesday

11 Thursday

12 Friday

13 Saturday

Last Quarter

14 Sunday

Long cushion cover. Silk velvet with applied linen canvas, embroidered with silk and metal thread in tent stitch and laid and couched work. English, about 1600.

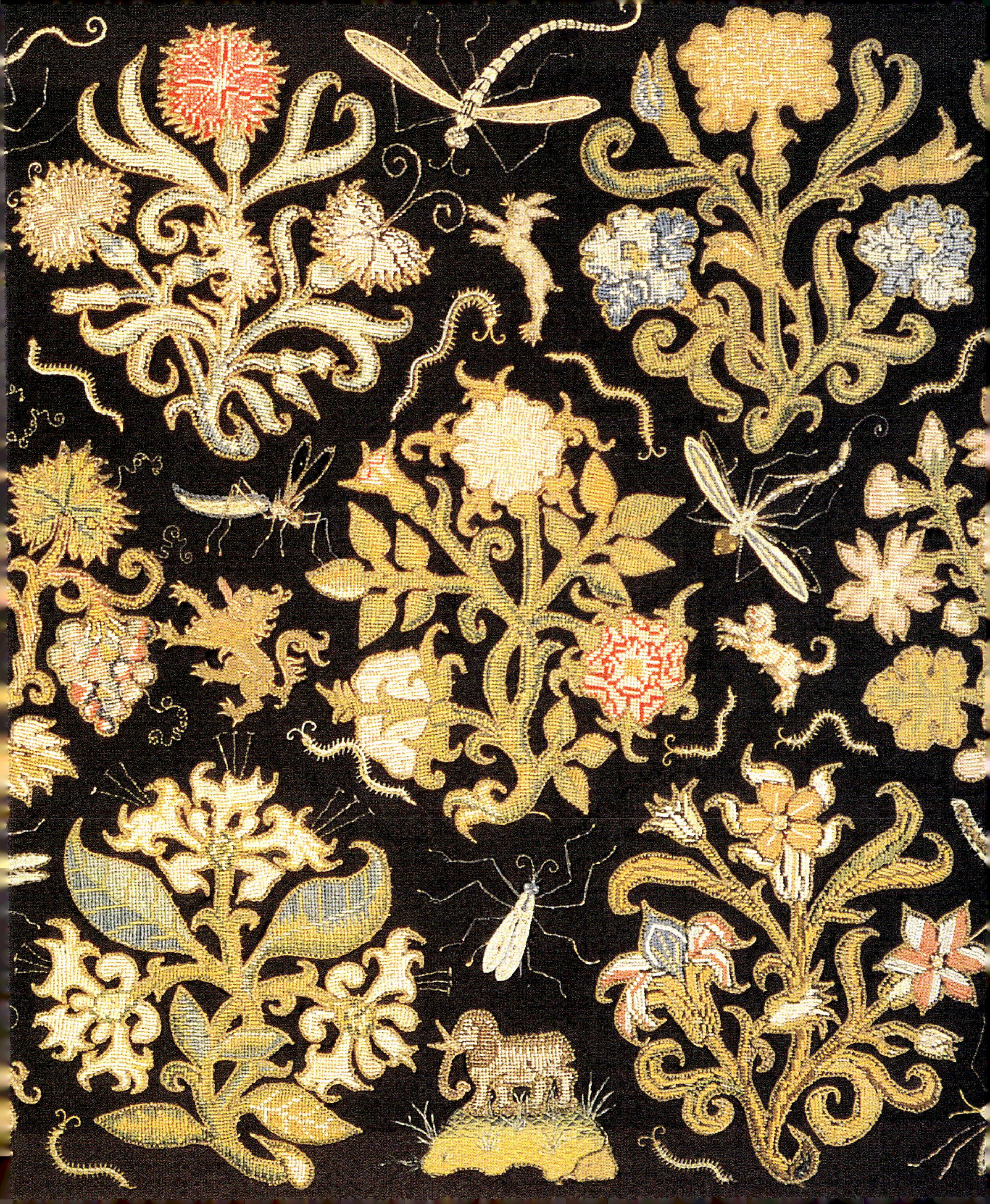

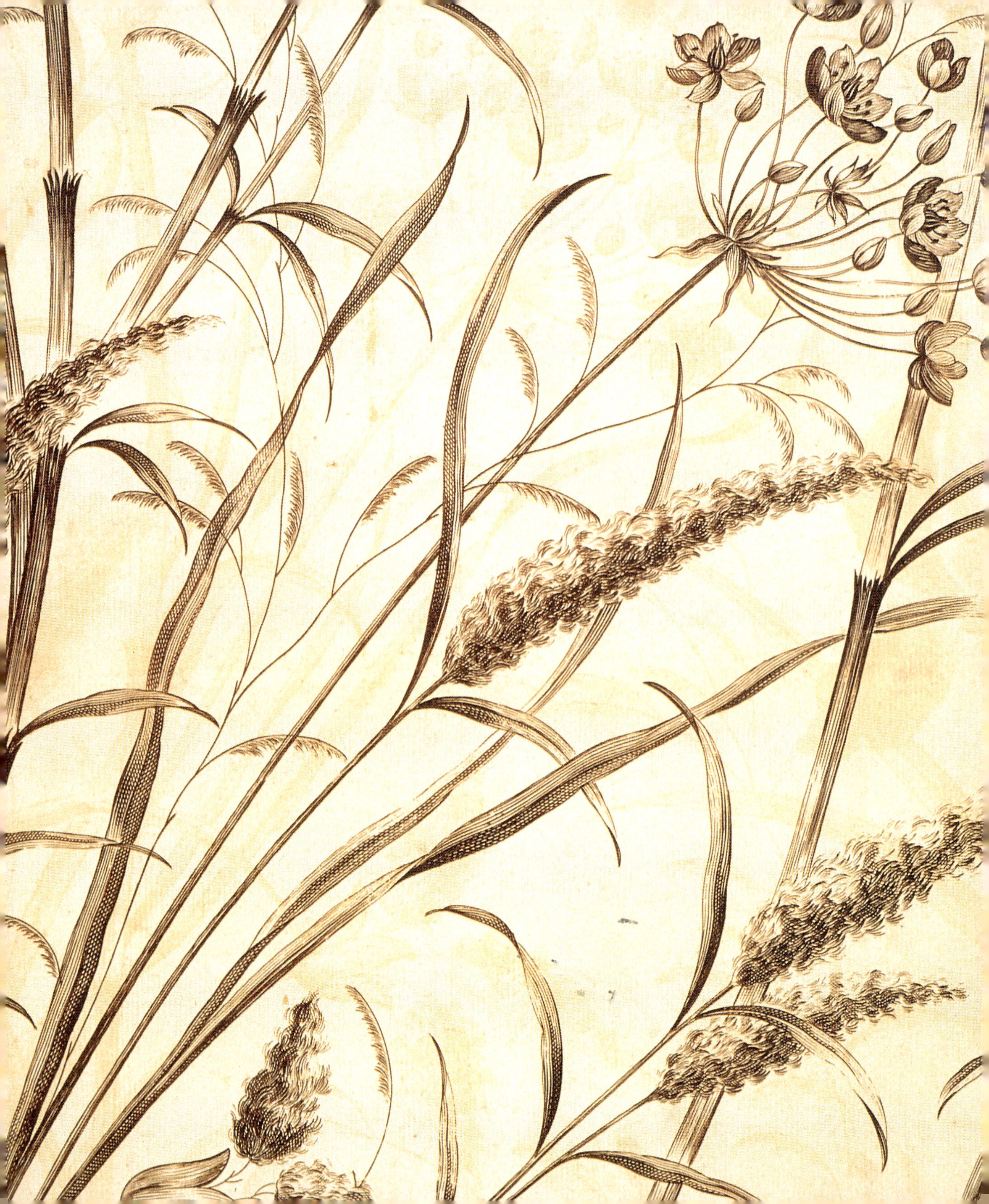

WEEK 12 — March

Monday 15

Tuesday 16

Country ? ? 11.30
Lunch 1.30. Forrester Brown.

Wednesday 17

Hospice 10.30.

St Patrick's Day
Holiday, Northern Ireland and Republic of Ireland

Thursday 18

Christine 9am.
Hubbels 12.0.

Friday 19

Mama died 2.5yrs - 3yrs
my Colm op!

Saturday 20

New Moon
Vernal Equinox

Sunday 21

1st day of Spring..

Mothering Sunday, UK

Page from the Bromley Hall pattern book of printed textile designs. Impression on paper from a copper plate. English, 1760–1800.

March

a Garnet Lasting Night-gown

WEEK 13

22 Monday

23 Tuesday
Nicolas Allday.

24 Wednesday
Mr Hawerden 10.25.

25 Thursday

26 Friday
Hair 1.30.
Choir Practice

27 Saturday

28 Sunday
Pilcombe

First Quarter
British Summer Time begins

Cuttings of dress fabrics, including printed fashion sources, put together by Barbara Johnson. English, 1767–1768.

five and ninepence a yard.
four dozen and half of
trimming. 5:6 a dozen.
Stamford Races. June. 1767.

a dozen & half of trimming
five & sixpence a dozen
1767

Lottery Ticket 24037

A Lady in the Court Dress of
the Year 1768.

The Undress.   The Brunswick.

a Garnet Lustring Night-gown
three qrs. wide. 1768:
nine yards. at 4:6 a yard

white Lustring Gown
five and sixpence a yard
eight yards. 3 qrs wide
1768

a purple and white

WEEK 14

March/April

Monday 29

Tuesday 30

Wednesday 31

Thursday 1

Friday 2

Saturday 3

Sunday 4

Palm Sunday

Printed cotton dress fabric, possibly designed by William Kilburn. English, 1787–1790.

April

WEEK 15

---

5 Monday

Full Moon

---

6 Tuesday

Passover (Pesach), First Day

---

7 Wednesday

---

8 Thursday

Maundy Thursday

---

9 Friday

Good Friday
Holiday, UK, Republic of Ireland, Canada, USA, Australia and New Zealand

---

10 Saturday

---

11 Sunday

Easter Sunday

Brocaded silk tobine dress fabric, woven in Spitalfields, London. English, 1760–1765.

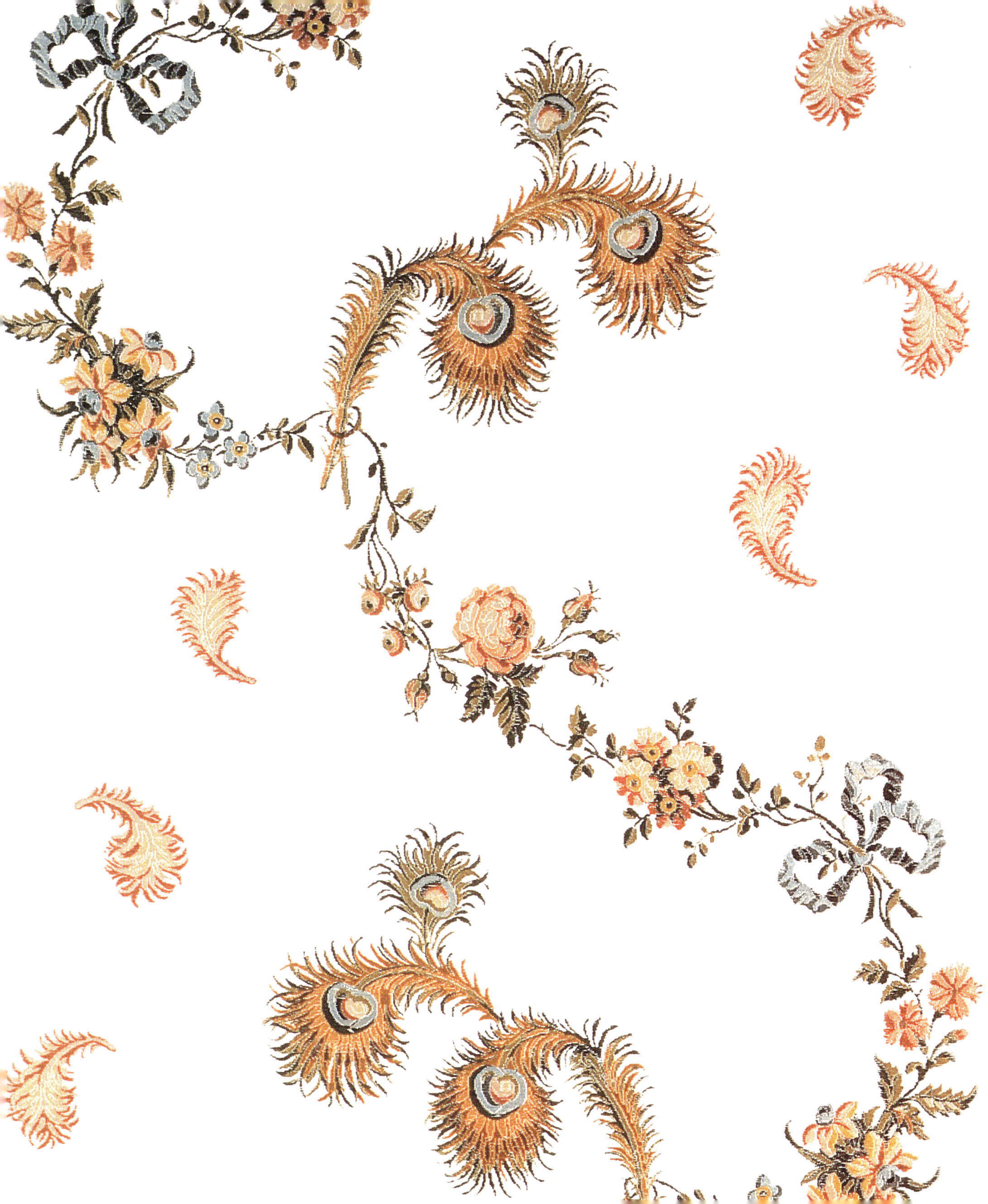

WEEK 16

April

Monday 12

Last Quarter
Easter Monday
Holiday, UK (exc. Scotland), Republic of Ireland, Canada, Australia and New Zealand
Passover (Pesach), Seventh Day

Tuesday 13

Passover (Pesach), Eighth Day

Wednesday 14

Thursday 15

Friday 16

Saturday 17

Sunday 18

Textile design for printed silk, from J.C. Robinson's Treasury of Ornamental Art. *English, 1857.*

April

WEEK 17

19 Monday *Feel Harry.*
Time to Shave ?.

New Moon

20 Tuesday

21 Wednesday

Birthday of Queen Elizabeth II

22 Thursday

23 Friday

St George's Day

24 Saturday

25 Sunday

Roller-printed, cotton furnishing fabric, printed by
Joseph Lockett for George Palfreyman, Manchester.
English, 1816–1820.

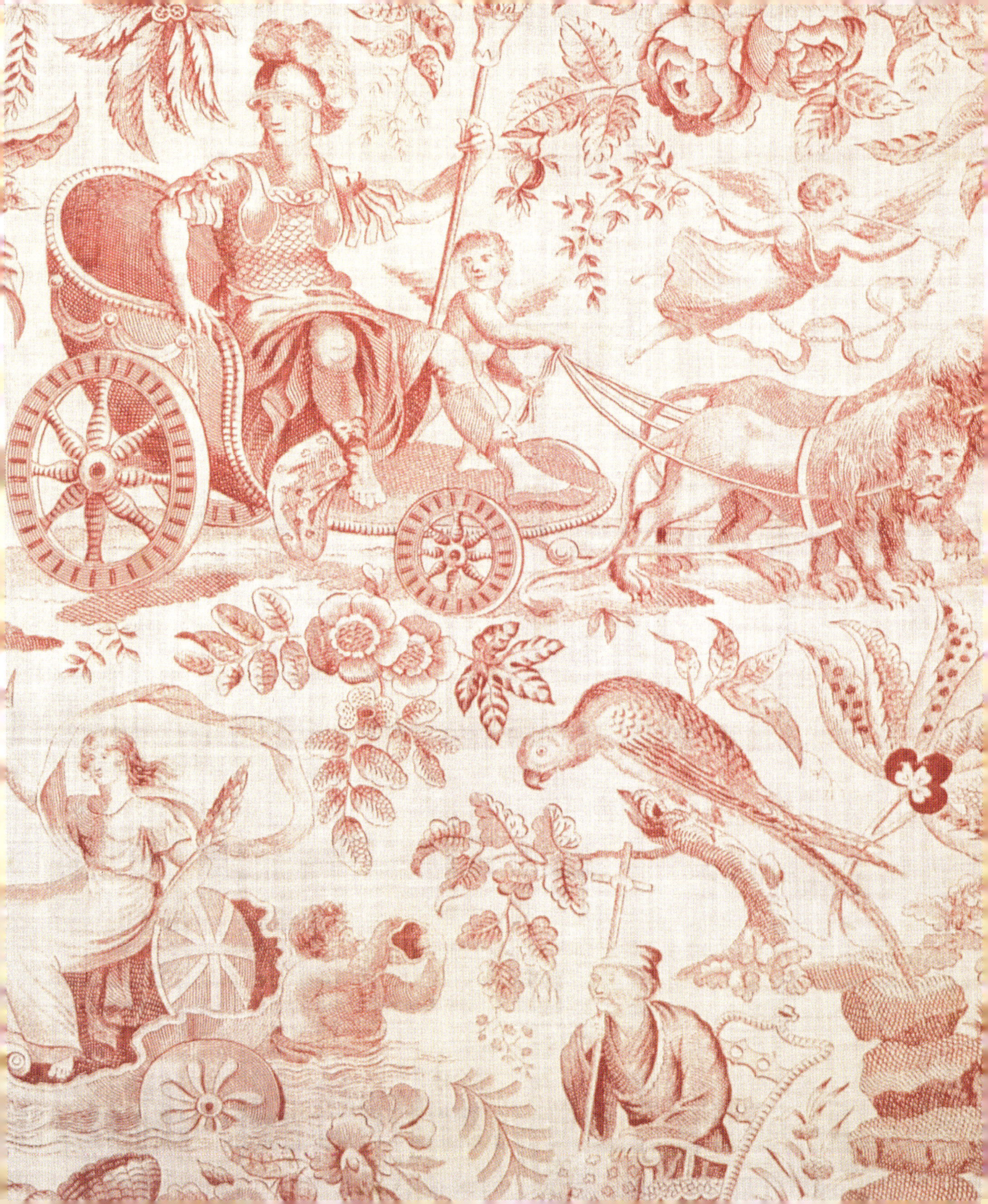

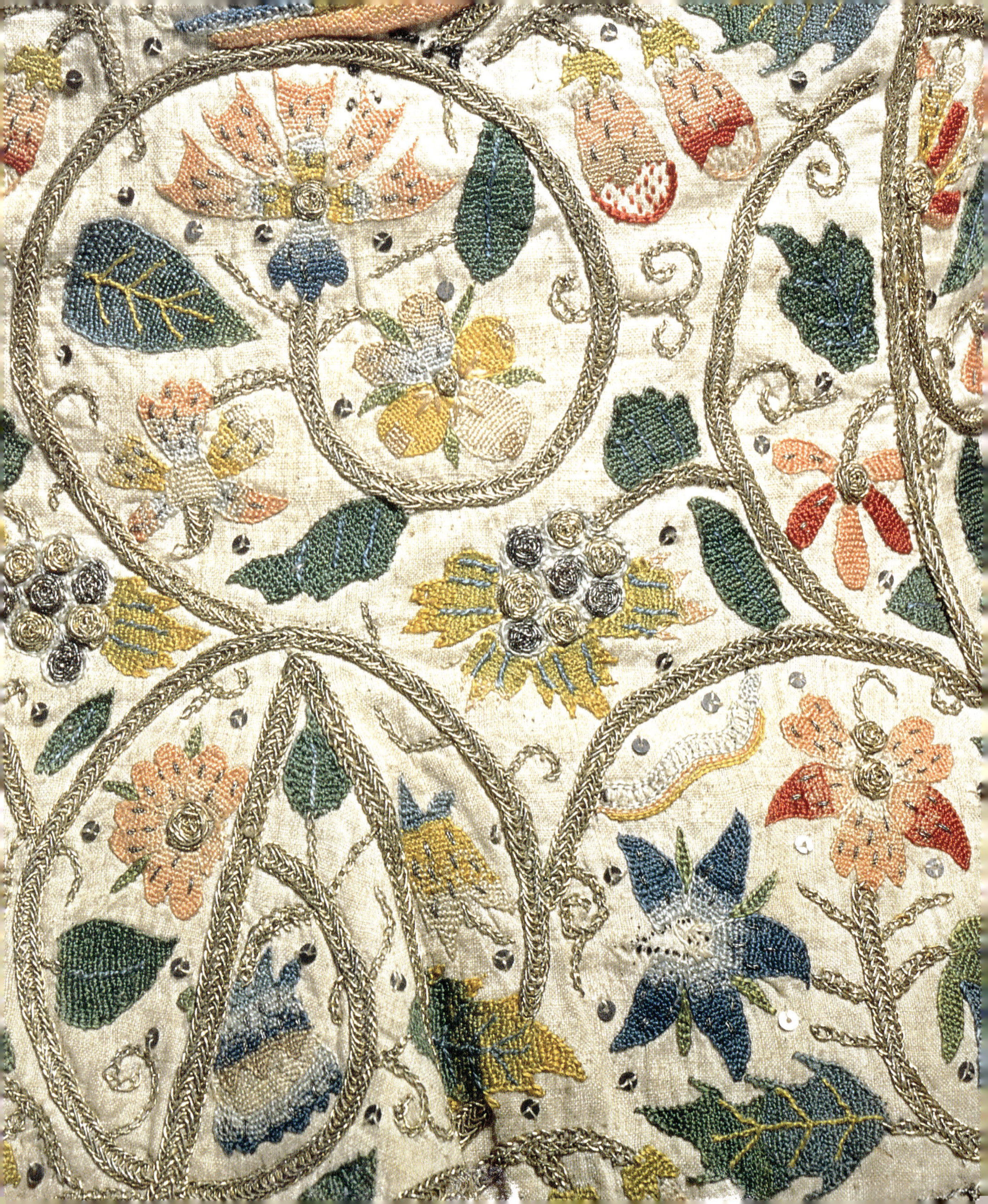

WEEK 18

April/May

Monday 26

Holiday, Australia and New Zealand (Anzac Day)

Tuesday 27

First Quarter

Wednesday 28

Thursday 29

Friday 30

Saturday 1

Sunday 2

Margaret Laton's jacket (detail). *Linen embroidered with silver and silver-gilt thread, coloured silks, bobbin lace and spangles (sequins). English, about 1610 (altered about 1620).*

May

WEEK 19

3 Monday

Early May Bank Holiday, UK and Republic of Ireland

4 Tuesday

Full Moon

5 Wednesday

6 Thursday

7 Friday

8 Saturday

9 Sunday

Mother's Day, Canada, USA, Australia and New Zealand

Chalice veil. Satin with patterning wefts of silver thread, woven in Spitalfields, London. English, about 1708.

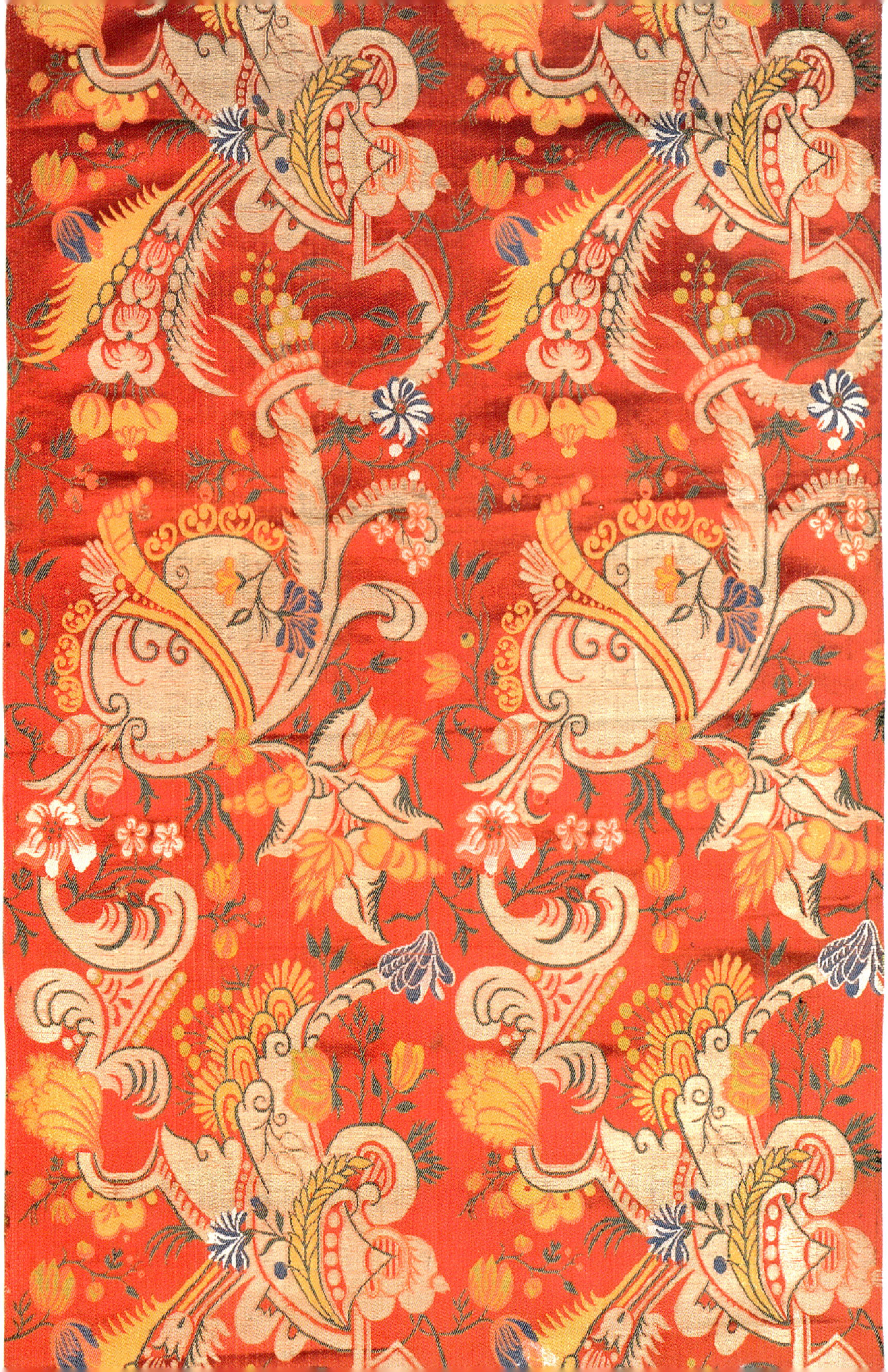

WEEK 20

May

Monday 10

Tuesday 11

Last Quarter

Wednesday 12

Thursday 13

Friday 14

Saturday 15

Sunday 16

Satin brocaded dress fabric with silks, silver and silver-gilt thread. French, 1705–1710.

May

WEEK 21

17 Monday

18 Tuesday

19 Wednesday

New Moon

20 Thursday

Ascension Day

21 Friday

22 Saturday

23 Sunday

Plate-printed, cotton furnishing fabric in china blue, using a copper plate engraved by Henry Roberts. Printed by Nixon & Co., Surrey (originally for John Collins at Woolmers, Hertfordshire). English, 1765.

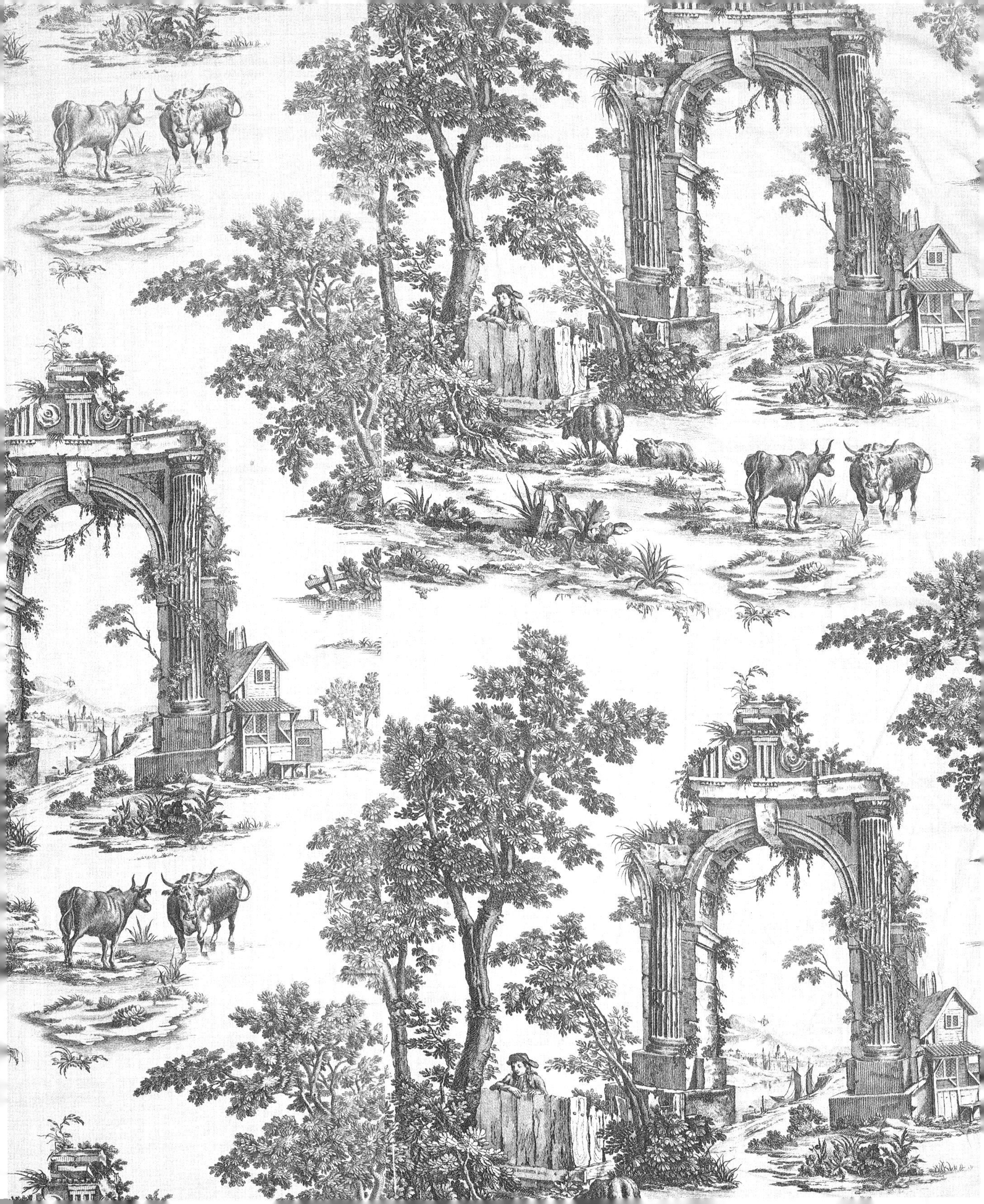

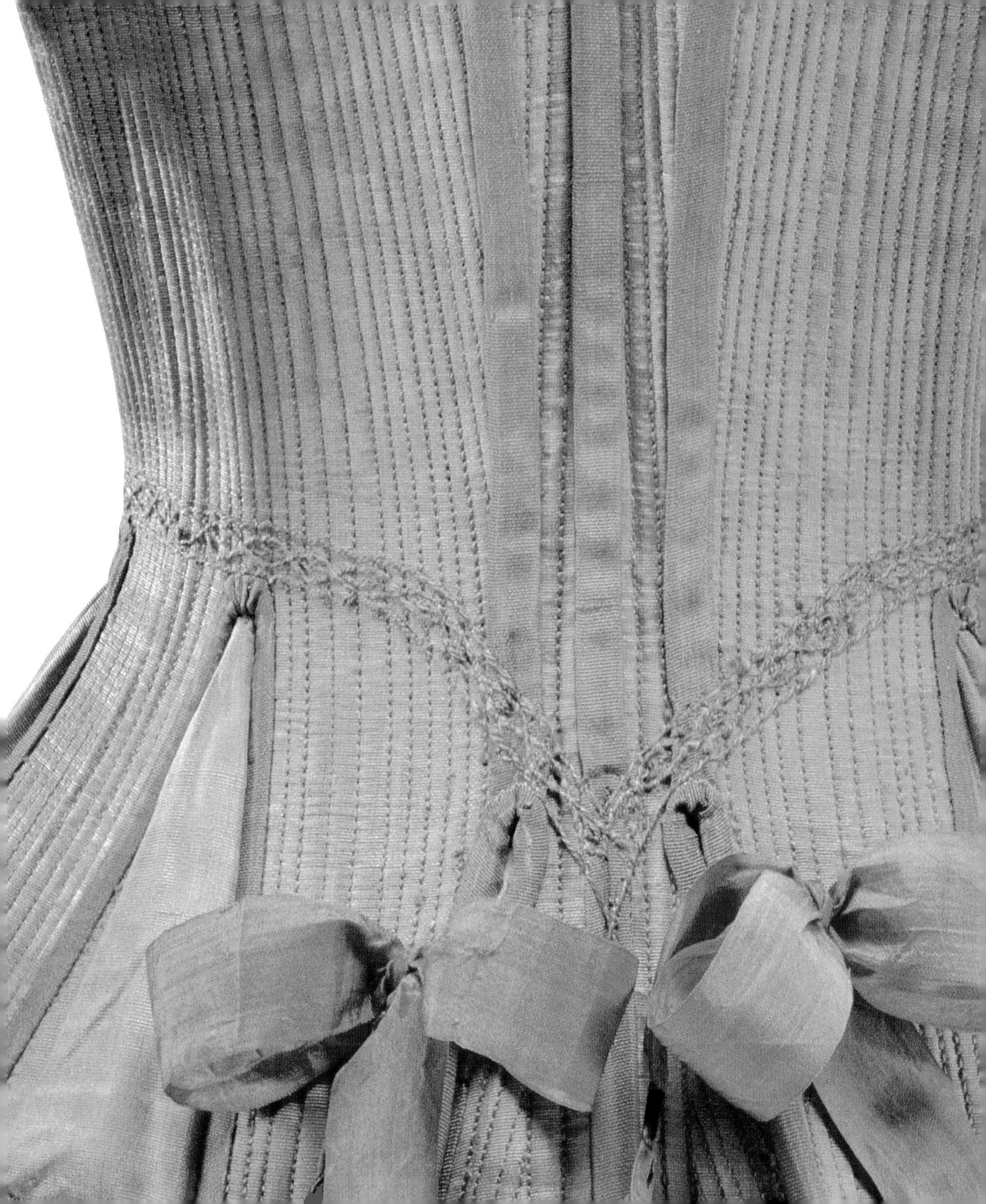

WEEK 22

May

Monday 24

Holiday, Canada (Victoria Day)

Tuesday 25

Wednesday 26

Jewish Feast of Weeks (Shavuot)

Thursday 27

First Quarter

Friday 28

Saturday 29

Sunday 30

Whit Sunday (Pentecost)

Pink silk stays. Watered silk, linen, whalebone and silk ribbons, probably made in England from English and Italian silk, 1660–1670.

May/June

WEEK 23

31 Monday

Spring Bank Holiday, UK
Holiday, USA (Memorial Day)

1 Tuesday

2 Wednesday

3 Thursday

Full moon

4 Friday

5 Saturday

6 Sunday

Trinity Sunday

Dress silk. Taffeta brocaded in silver thread. Woven in Spitalfields from a Anna Maria Garthwaite design. English, 1742.

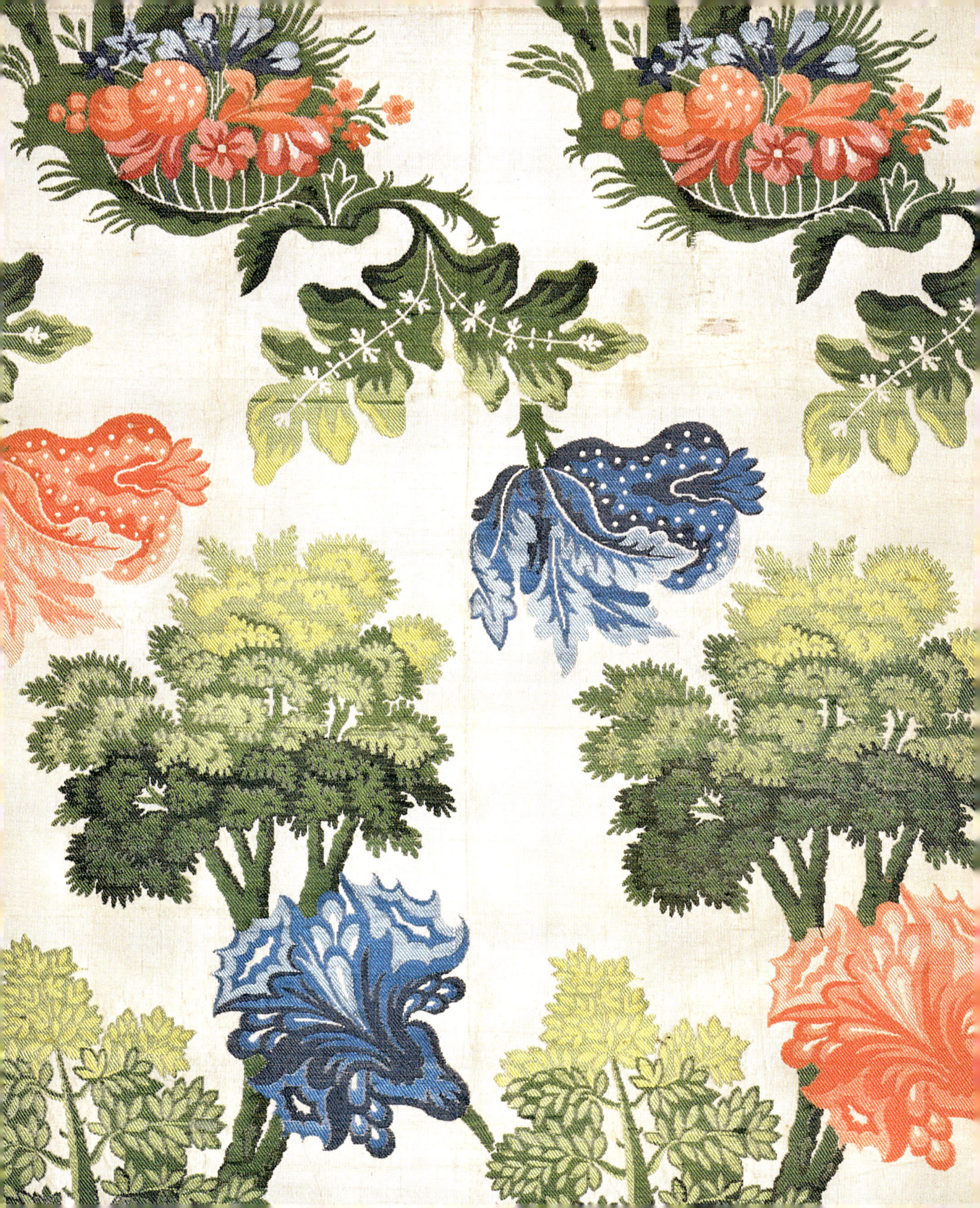

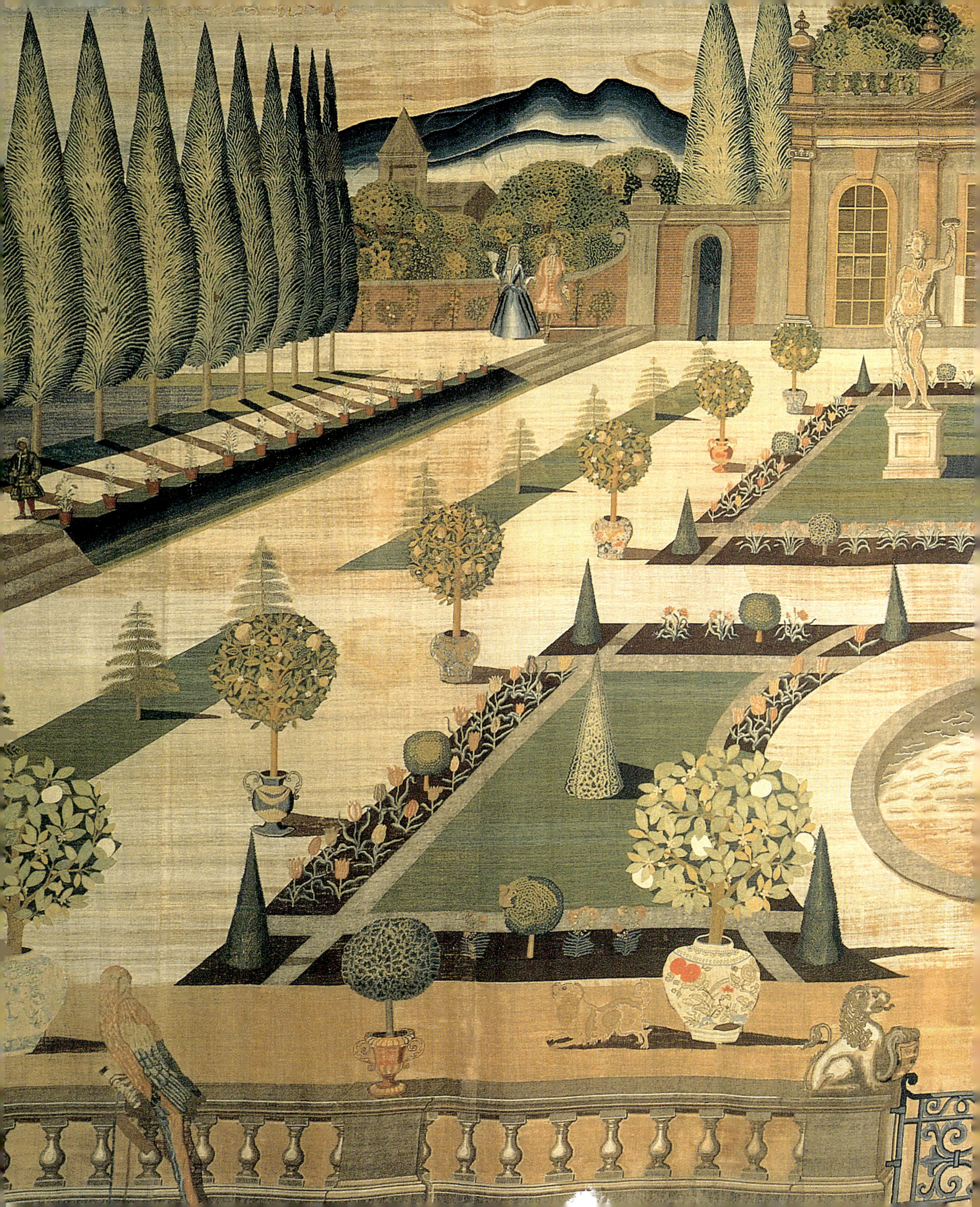

WEEK 24 | June

Monday 7

Holiday, New Zealand (The Queen's birthday)

Tuesday 8

Wednesday 9

Last Quarter

Thursday 10

Corpus Christi

Friday 11

Saturday 12

The Queen's official birthday (subject to confirmation)

Sunday 13

Embroidery from Stoke Edith, Herefordshire. Linen canvas embroidered with silk and wool, with some details in appliqué. English, 1710–1720.

June

WEEK 25

14 Monday

Holiday, Australia (The Queen's birthday)

15 Tuesday

16 Wednesday

17 Thursday

New Moon

18 Friday

19 Saturday

20 Sunday

Father's Day, UK, Canada and USA

Cuttings of dress fabrics, including printed fashion sources, put together by Barbara Johnson. English, 1746–1749.

half a Guinea a yard

a Blue damask coat 1746
half a Guinea a yard

a flower'd cotton Jacket 1747

a blue & white linnen long sack 1748

a flower'd silk Robe-coat 1748

a Green Camblet coat 1749

a Flower'd Silk coat
7 = 6 a yard.

JUBILEE
1887

WEEK 26

June

Monday 21

Summer Solstice

Tuesday 22

Wednesday 23

Thursday 24

Friday 25

First Quarter

Saturday 26

Sunday 27

Commemorative, Golden Jubilee, roller-printed cotton, with repeating portrait of Queen Victoria. English, 1887.

June/July

WEEK 27

28 Monday

29 Tuesday

30 Wednesday

1 Thursday

Holiday, Canada (Canada Day)

2 Friday

Full Moon

3 Saturday

4 Sunday

Independence Day, USA

'Strawberry Thief' furnishing fabric. Indigo discharge and block-printed cotton. Designed and made by William Morris, Morris & Co. English, 1883.

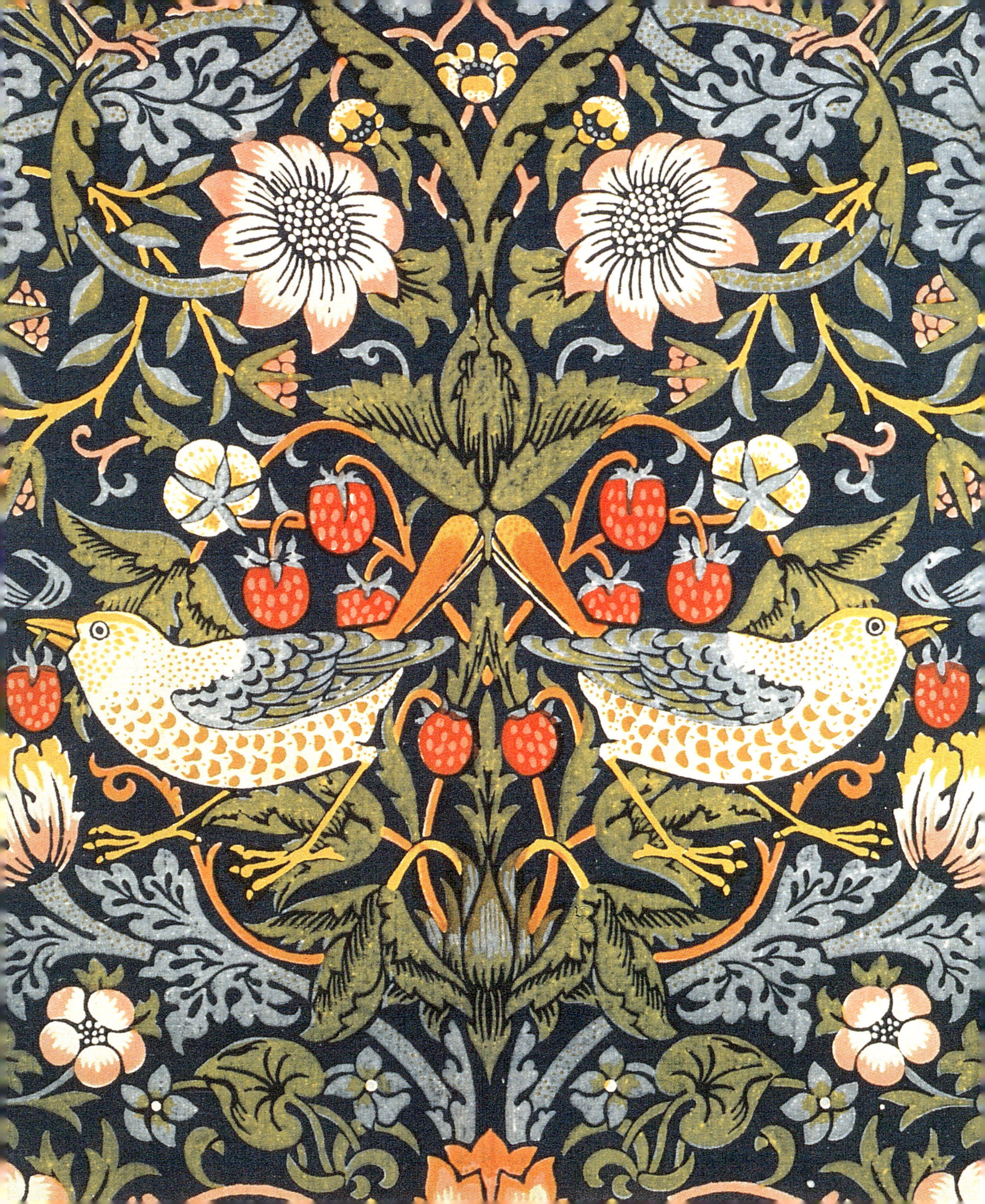

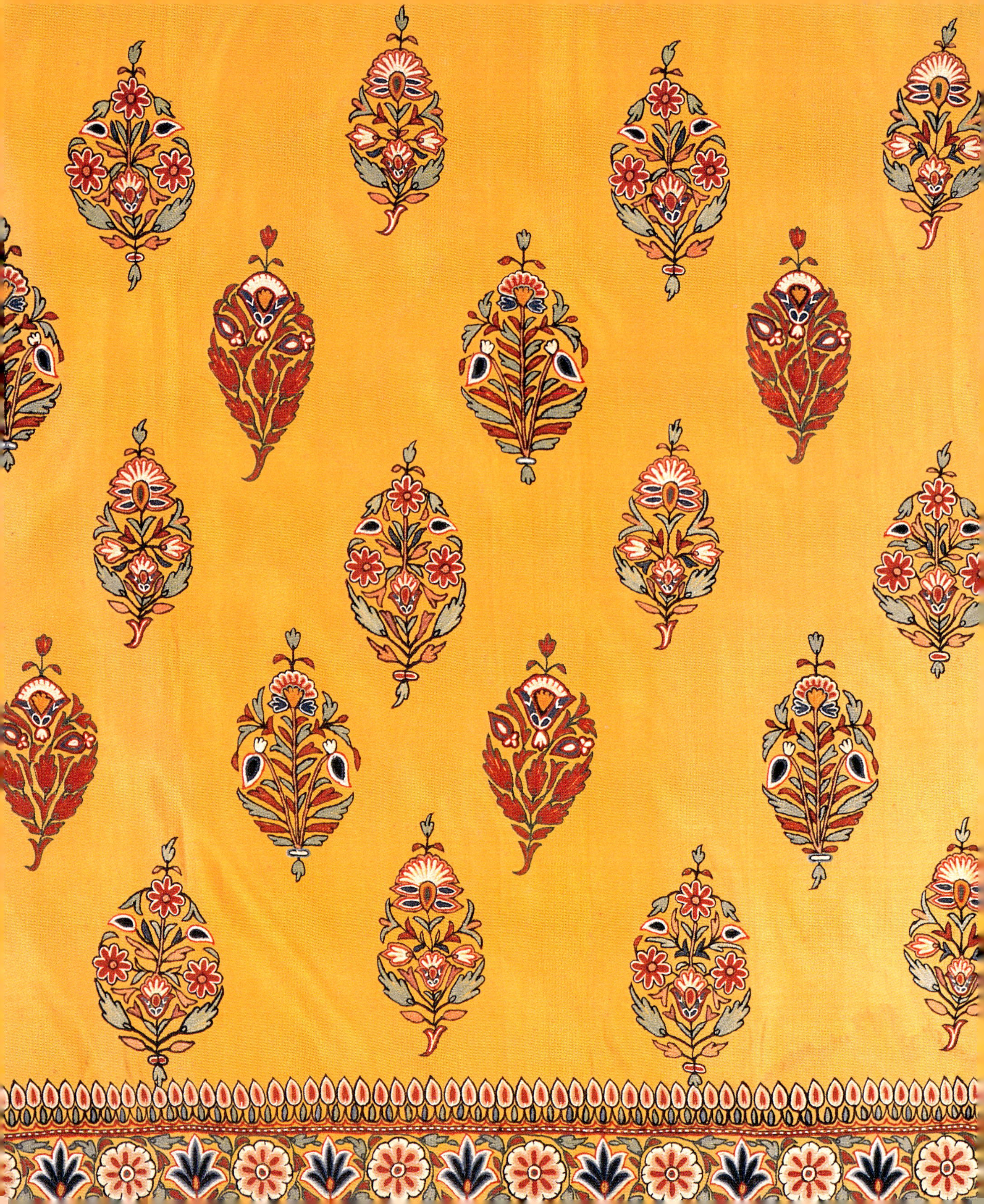

WEEK 28

July

Monday 5

Holiday, USA (Independence Day)

Tuesday 6

Wednesday 7

Thursday 8

Friday 9

Last Quarter

Saturday 10

Sunday 11

Skirt length. Silk satin ground embroidered in chain stitch with silk thread. Indian, about 1850.

July

WEEK 29

12 Monday

Holiday, Northern Ireland (Battle of the Boyne)

13 Tuesday

14 Wednesday

15 Thursday

St Swithin's Day

16 Friday

17 Saturday

New Moon

18 Sunday

Palampore (bed cover). Painted and dyed cotton chintz. Made in south-east India, about 1750.

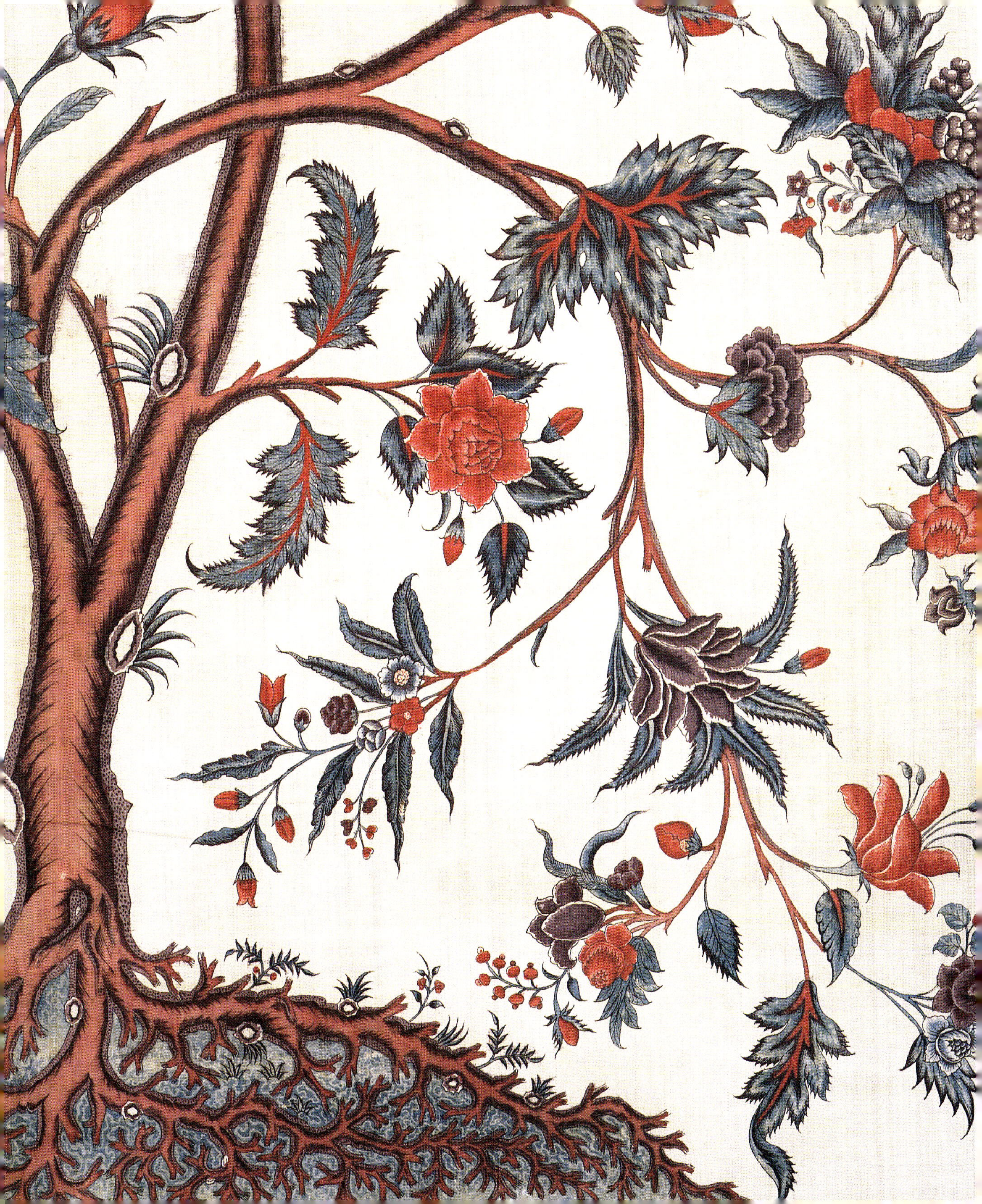

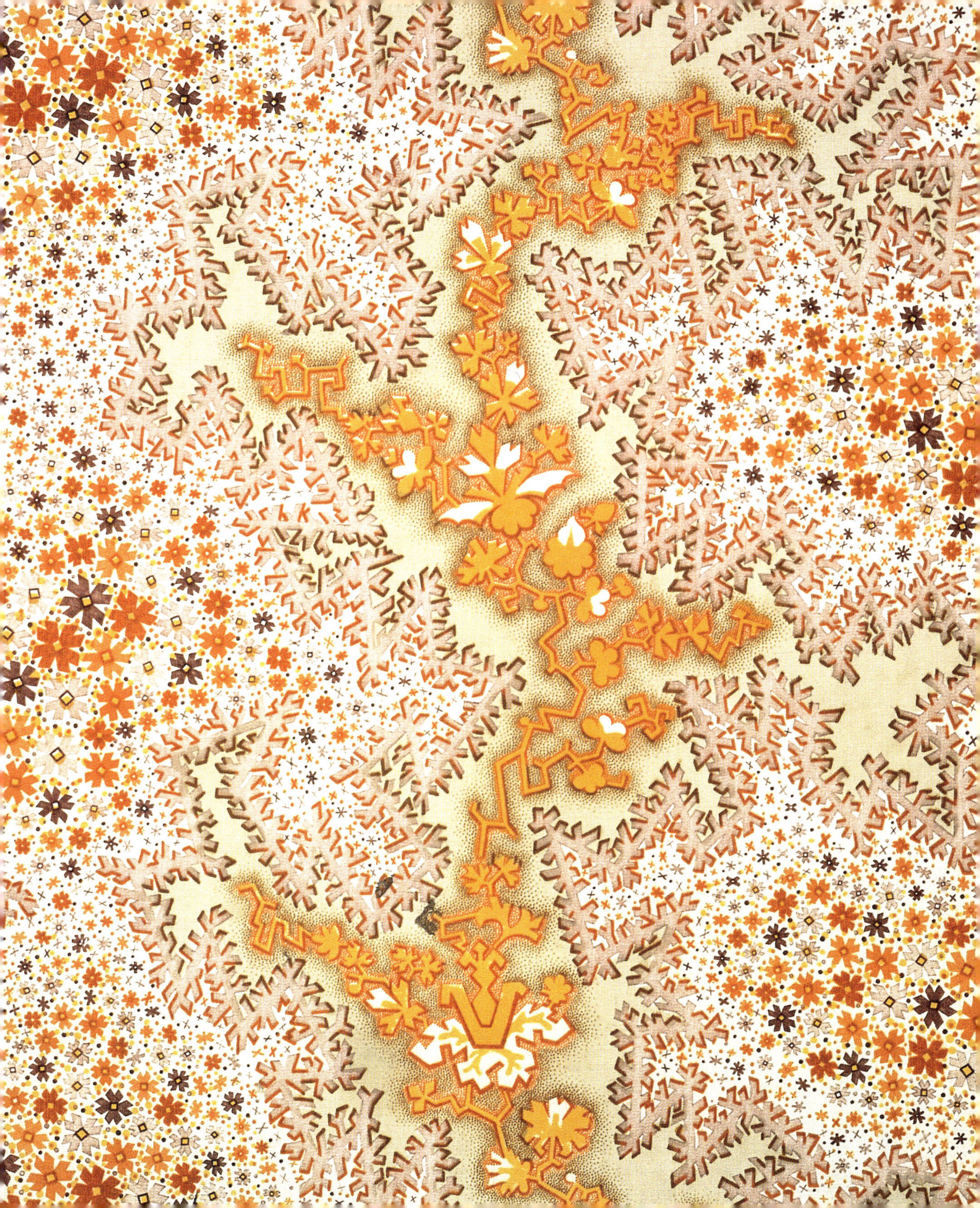

WEEK 30

July

Monday 19

Tuesday 20

Wednesday 21

Thursday 22

Friday 23

Saturday 24

Sunday 25

First Quarter

Roller-printed, cotton furnishing fabric, with extra colours added by surface roller. Printed in Lancashire. English, 1831.

July/August

WEEK 31

26 Monday

27 Tuesday

28 Wednesday

29 Thursday

30 Friday

31 Saturday

Full Moon

1 Sunday

Hanging, embroidered in crewel with wool on a linen ground. English, about 1700–1750.

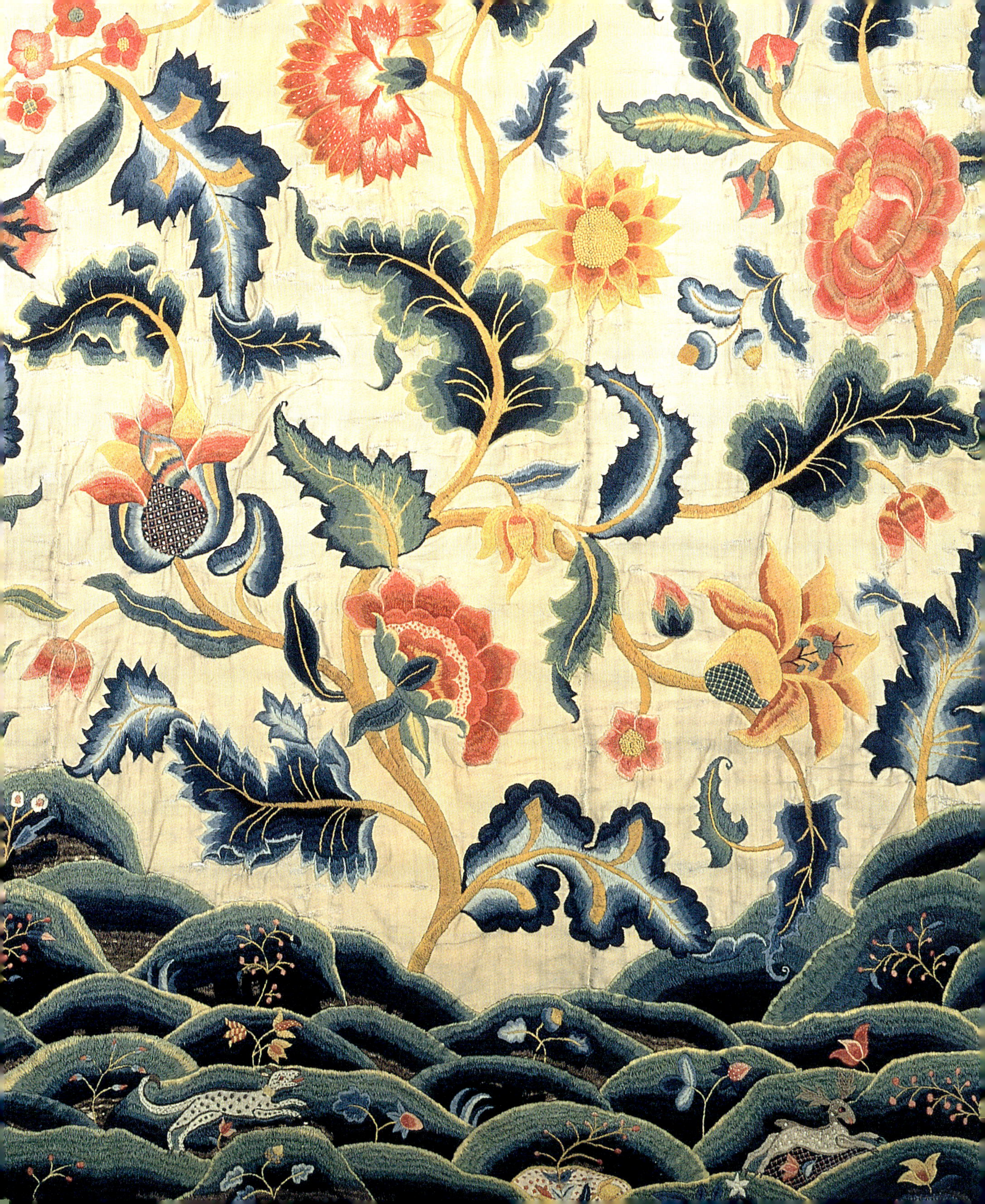

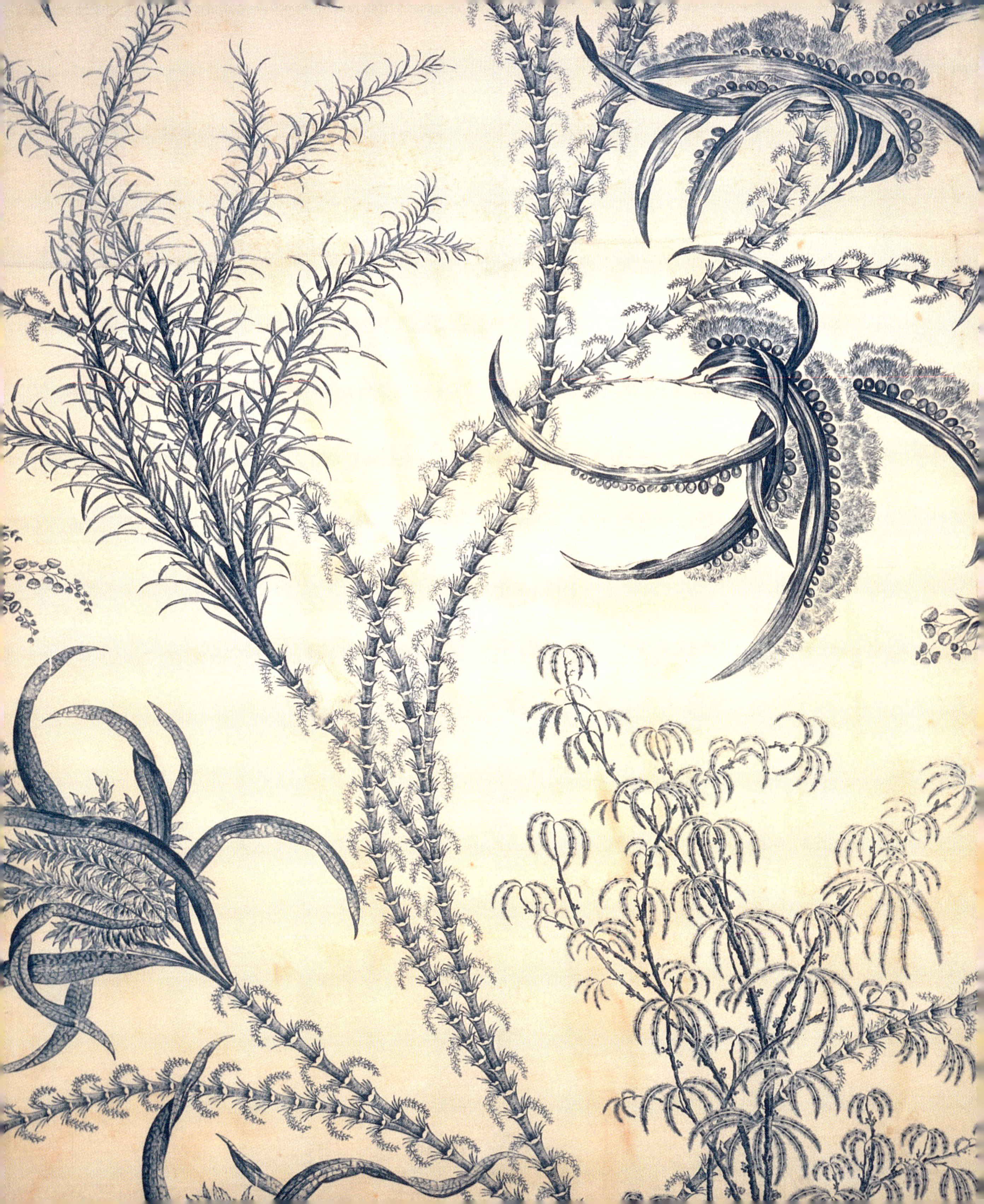

WEEK 32

August

Monday 2

Summer Bank Holiday, Scotland and Republic of Ireland

Tuesday 3

Wednesday 4

Thursday 5

Friday 6

Saturday 7

Last Quarter

Sunday 8

Cotton furnishing fabric, printed from engraved copper plates. Made by the firm of Ollive & Talwin, Bromley Hall, near London. English, about 1780.

August

WEEK 33

9 Monday

10 Tuesday

11 Wednesday

12 Thursday

13 Friday

14 Saturday

15 Sunday

Roller-printed, cotton furnishing fabric, with additional colours added by surface roller. Design taken from Audubon's The Birds of America. *Printed in Lancashire. English, 1830.*

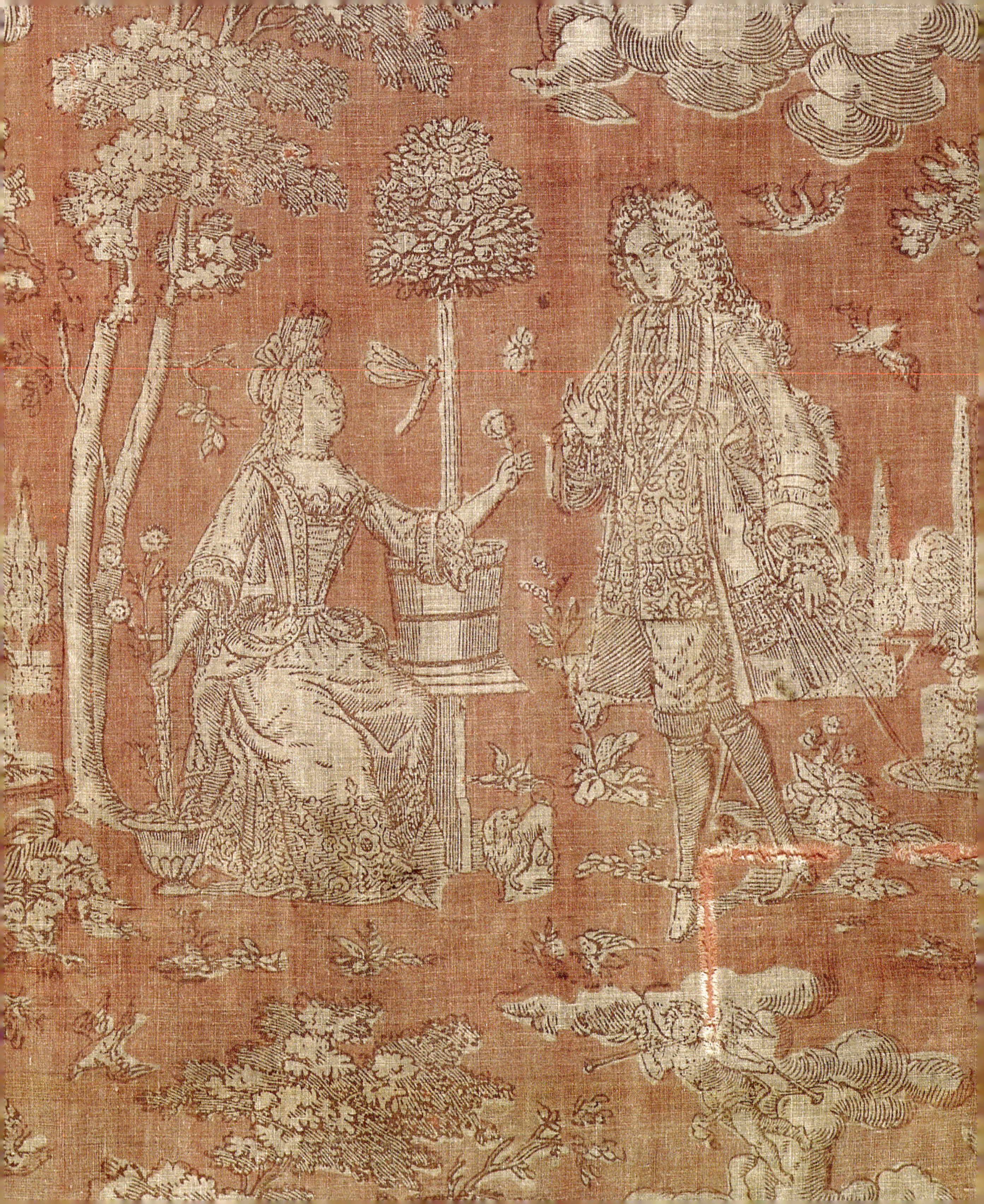

WEEK 34

August

Monday 16

New Moon

Tuesday 17

Wednesday 18

Thursday 19

Friday 20

Saturday 21

Sunday 22

Block-printed, cotton furnishing fabric.
Dutch, 1650–1699.

August

WEEK 35

23 Monday

First Quarter

24 Tuesday

25 Wednesday

26 Thursday

27 Friday

28 Saturday

29 Sunday

Abigail Pett's bed hanging, embroidered in crewel wool on a linen and cotton ground. English, 1680–1700.

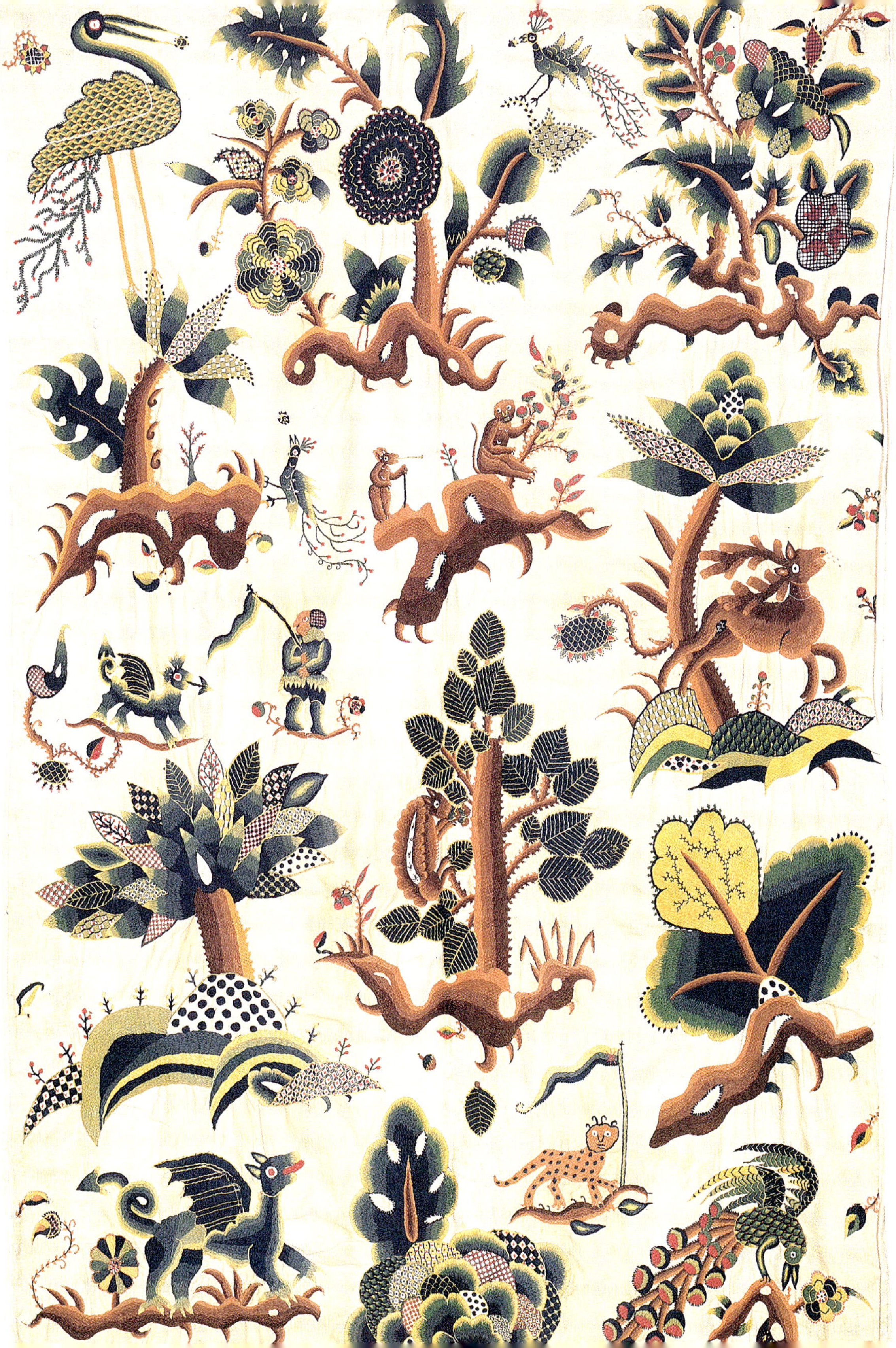

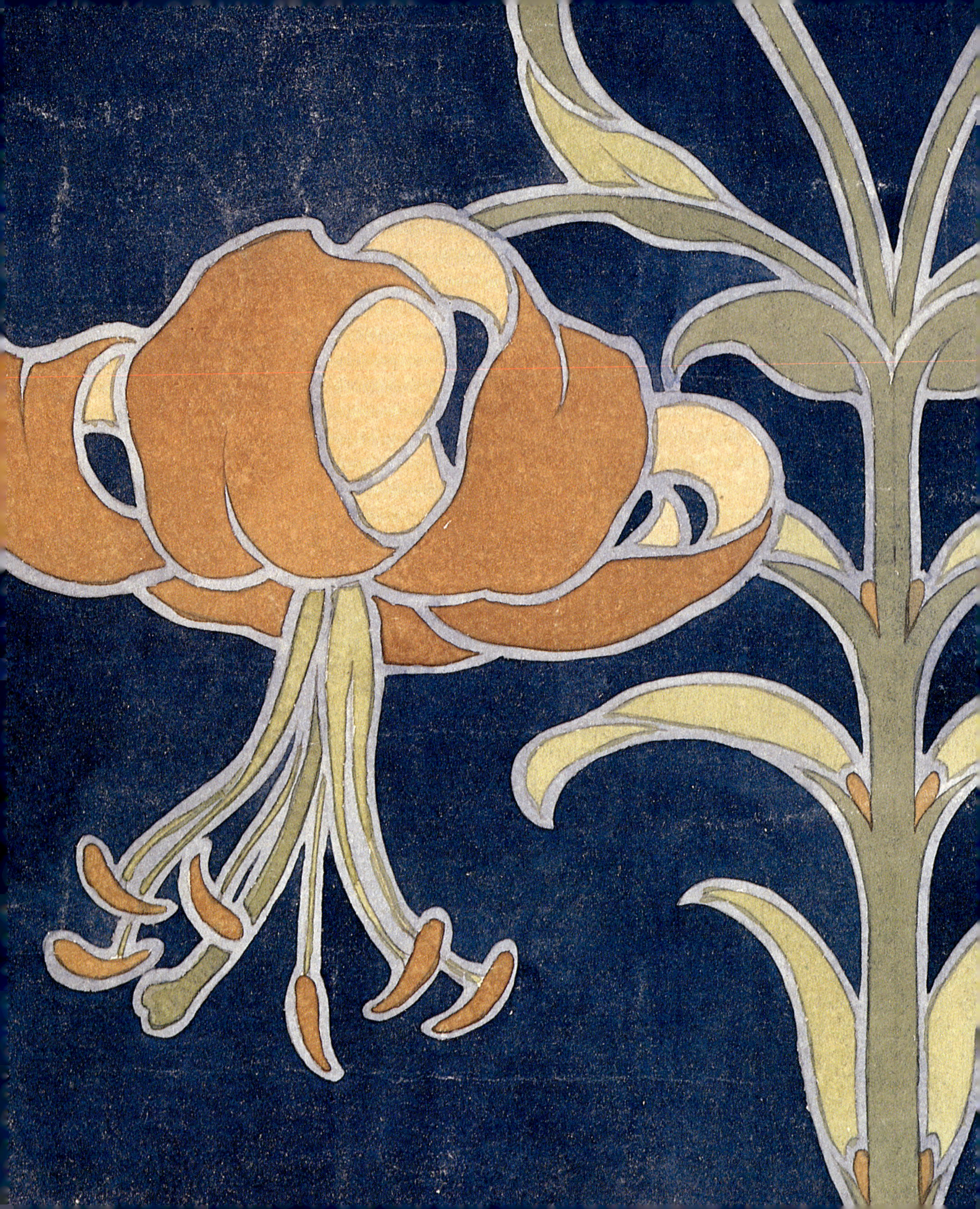

WEEK 36 — August/September

Monday 30

Full Moon
Summer Bank Holiday, UK (exc. Scotland)

Tuesday 31

Wednesday 1

Thursday 2

Friday 3

Saturday 4

Sunday 5

Father's Day, Australia and New Zealand

'Tiger Lily', *design for a printed textile by Lindsey P. Butterfield. Pencil and watercolour on paper. English, 1896.*

September

WEEK 37

6 Monday

Last Quarter
Holiday, Canada (Labour Day) and USA (Labor Day)

7 Tuesday

8 Wednesday

9 Thursday

10 Friday

11 Saturday

12 Sunday

Mirror frame (detail), showing Abraham asleep beneath a tree. Satin embroidered with silk thread (unfinished), raised and detached work. English, about 1650.

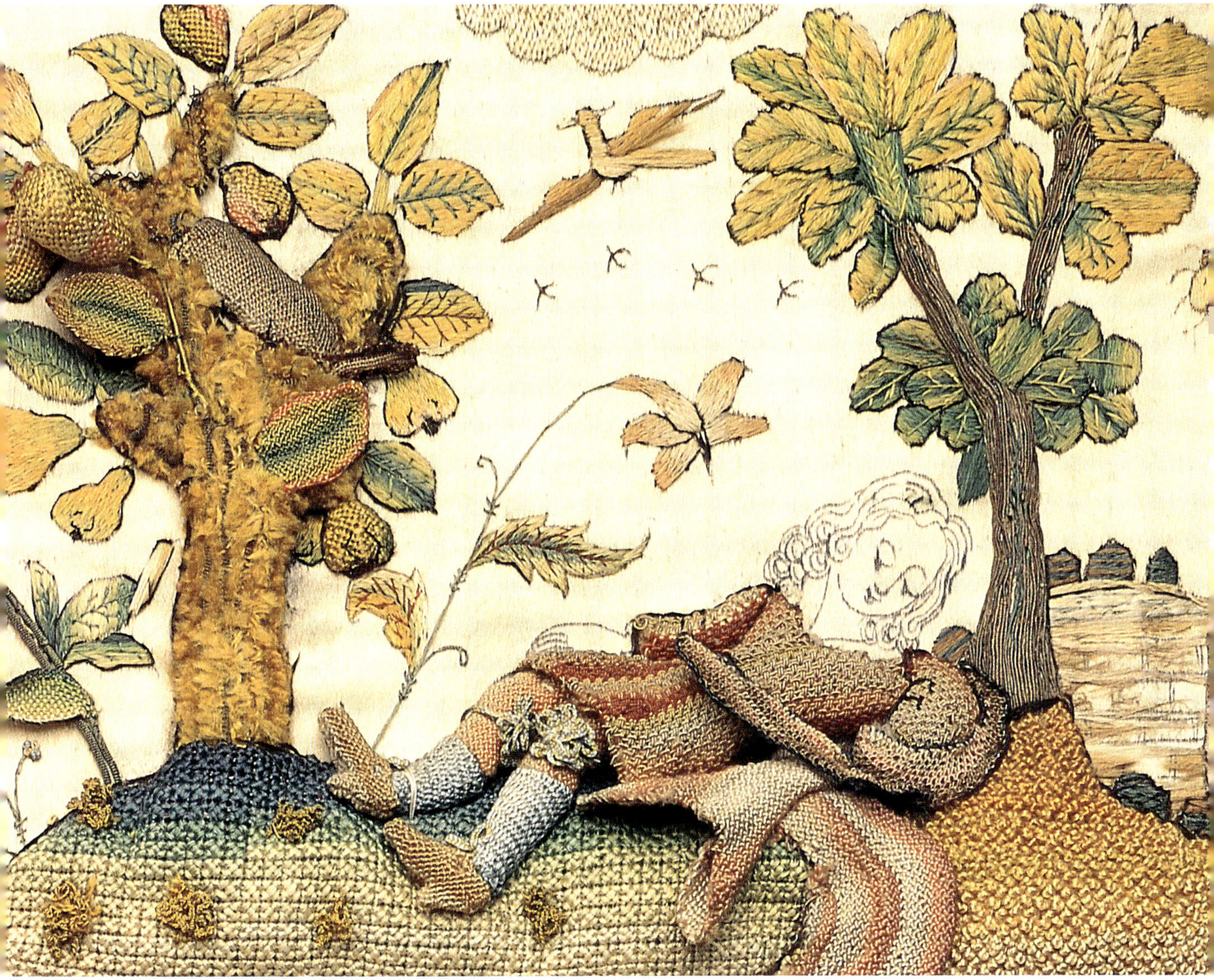

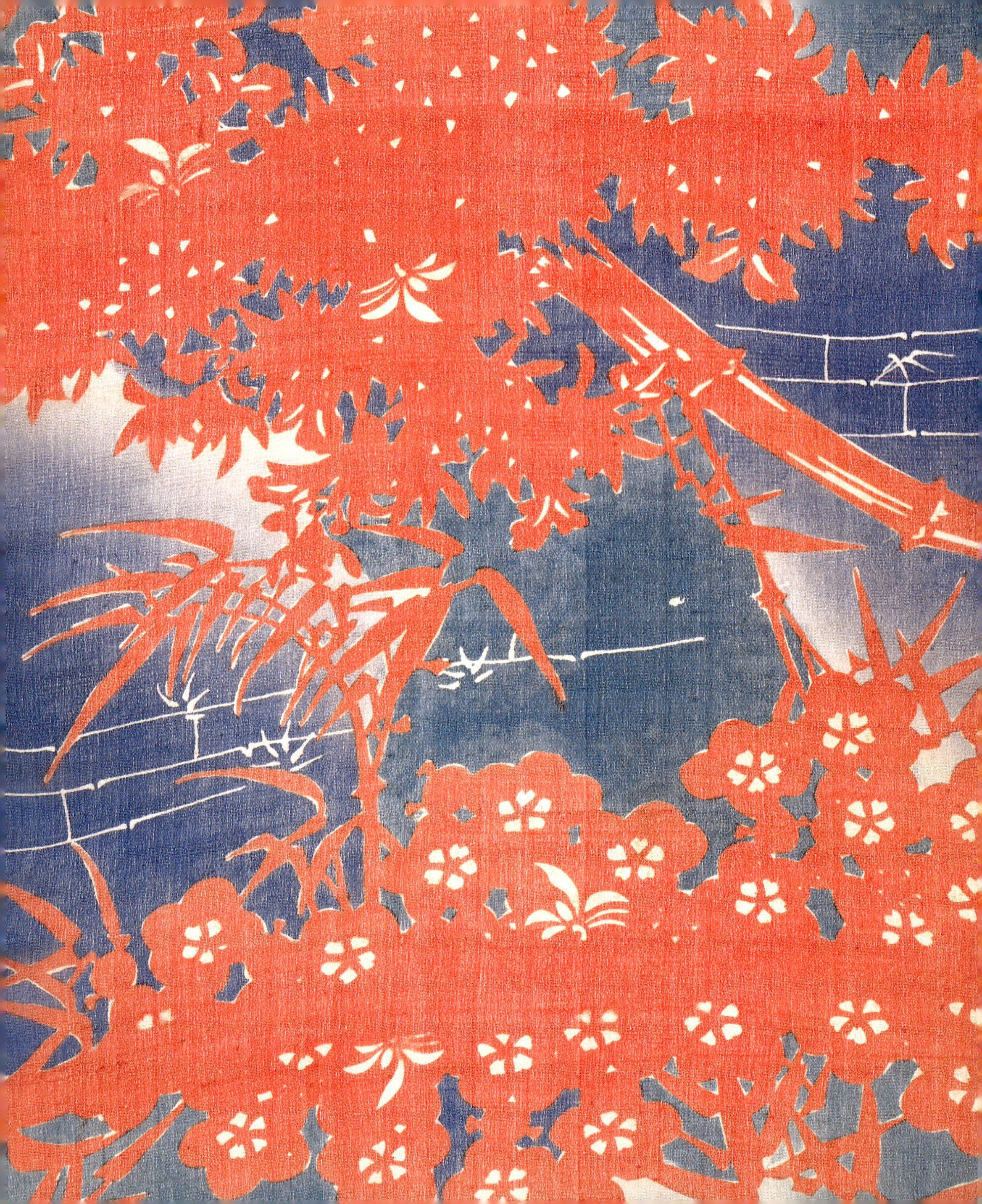

WEEK 38

September

Monday 13

Tuesday 14

New Moon

Wednesday 15

Thursday 16

Jewish New Year (Rosh Hashanah)

Friday 17

Saturday 18

Sunday 19

Length of resist-dyed crepe silk, decorated with stylised trees. Japanese, nineteenth century.

September

WEEK 39

20 Monday

21 Tuesday

First Quarter

22 Wednesday

Autumnal Equinox

23 Thursday

24 Friday

25 Saturday

Jewish Day of Atonement (Yom Kippur)

26 Sunday

Bed valance (detail), made for David Garrick and his wife. *Painted and dyed cotton chintz, produced in south-east India, about 1774.*

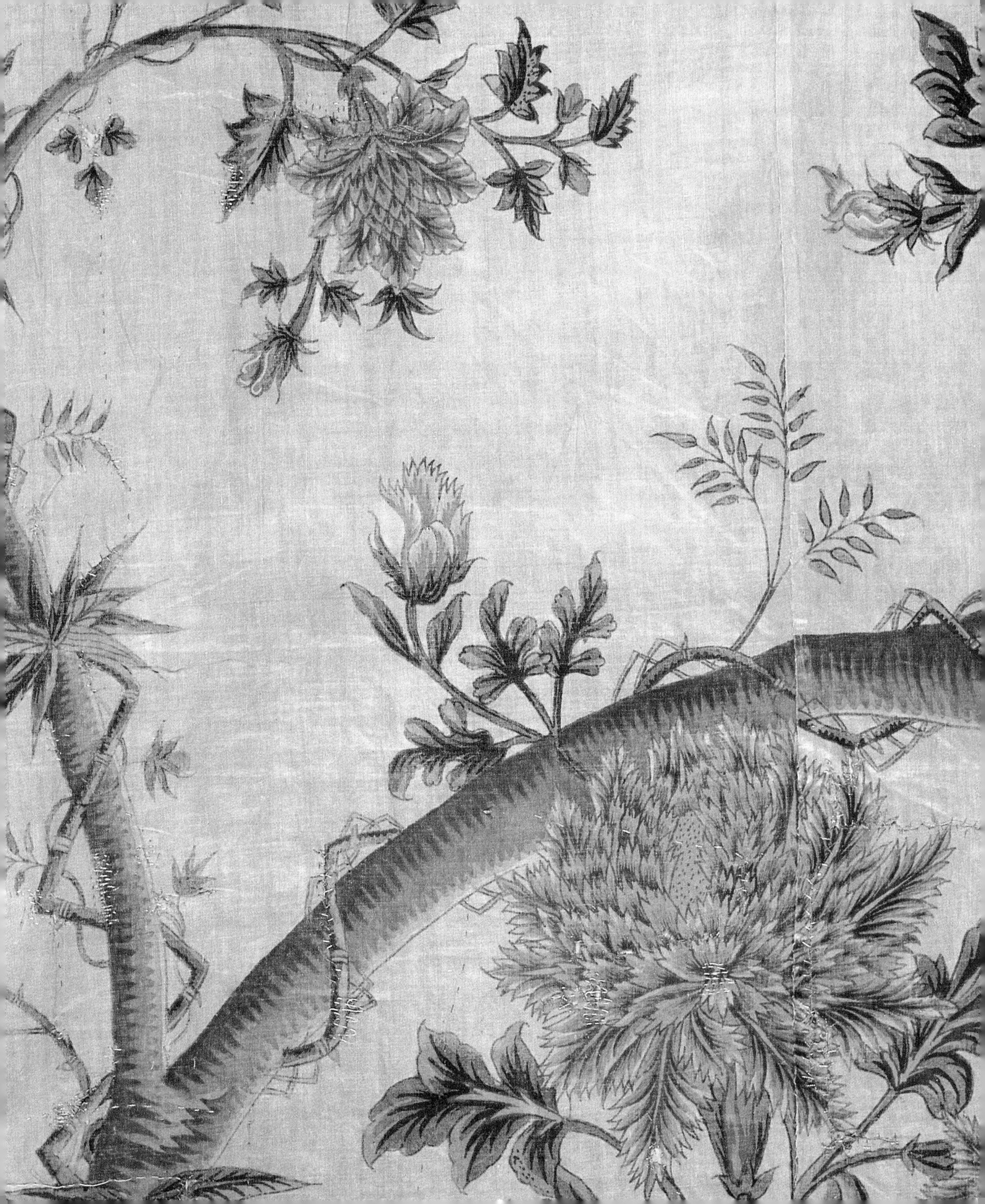

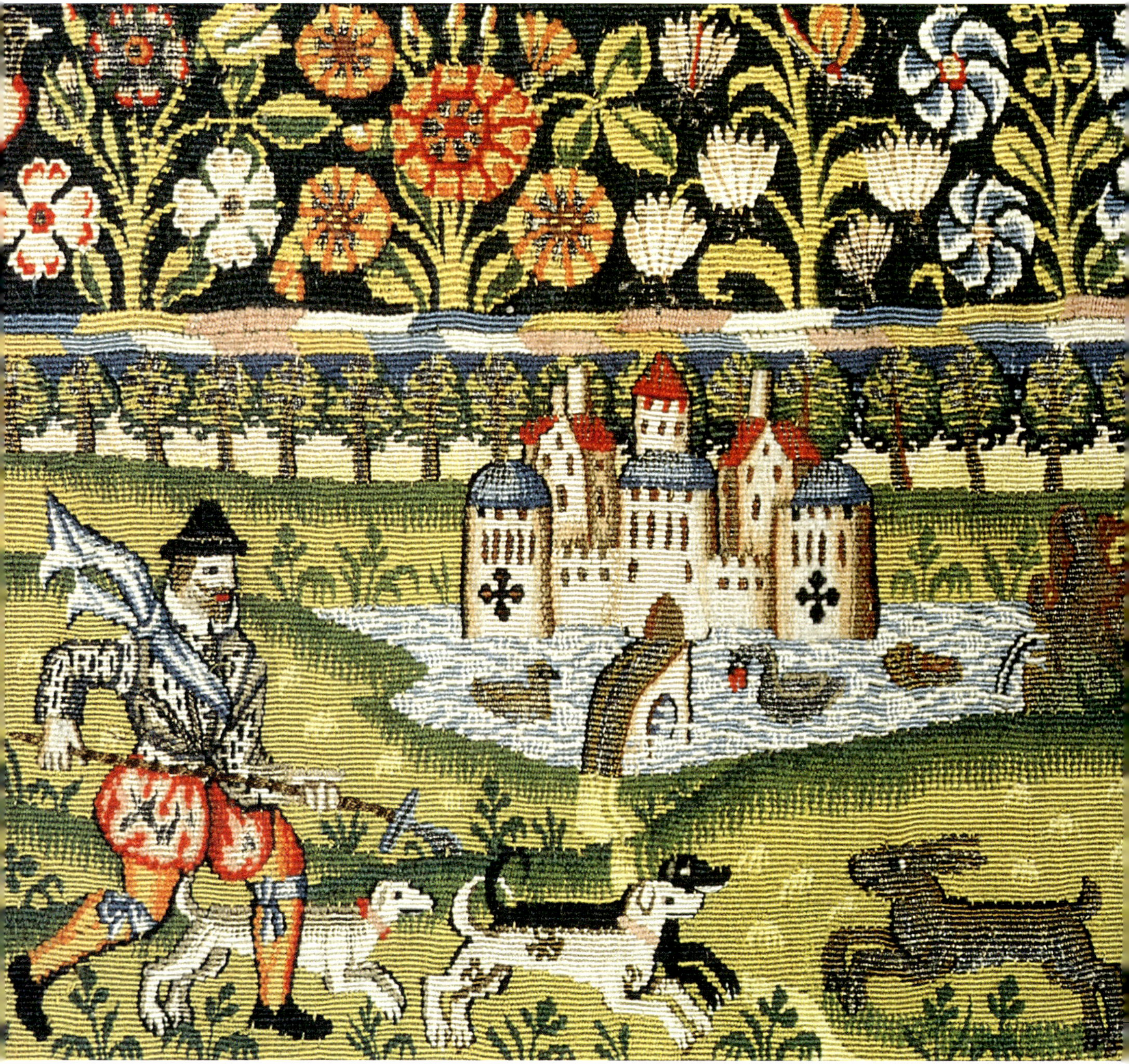

WEEK 40

September/October

Monday 27

Tuesday 28

Full Moon

Wednesday 29

Michaelmas Day

Thursday 30

Jewish Festival of Tabernacles (Succoth), First Day

Friday 1

Saturday 2

Sunday 3

Bed valance with hunting scenes. Tapestry, woven in silk and wool with some silver thread at the Sheldon Tapestry workshops. English, 1600–1610.

October

WEEK 41

4 Monday

5 Tuesday

6 Wednesday

Last Quarter
7 Thursday

Jewish Festival of Tabernacles (Succoth) Eighth Day
8 Friday

9 Saturday

10 Sunday

Silk and wool damask tablecloth, manufactured by Henry Walmsley & Co., Lancashire. English, 1851.

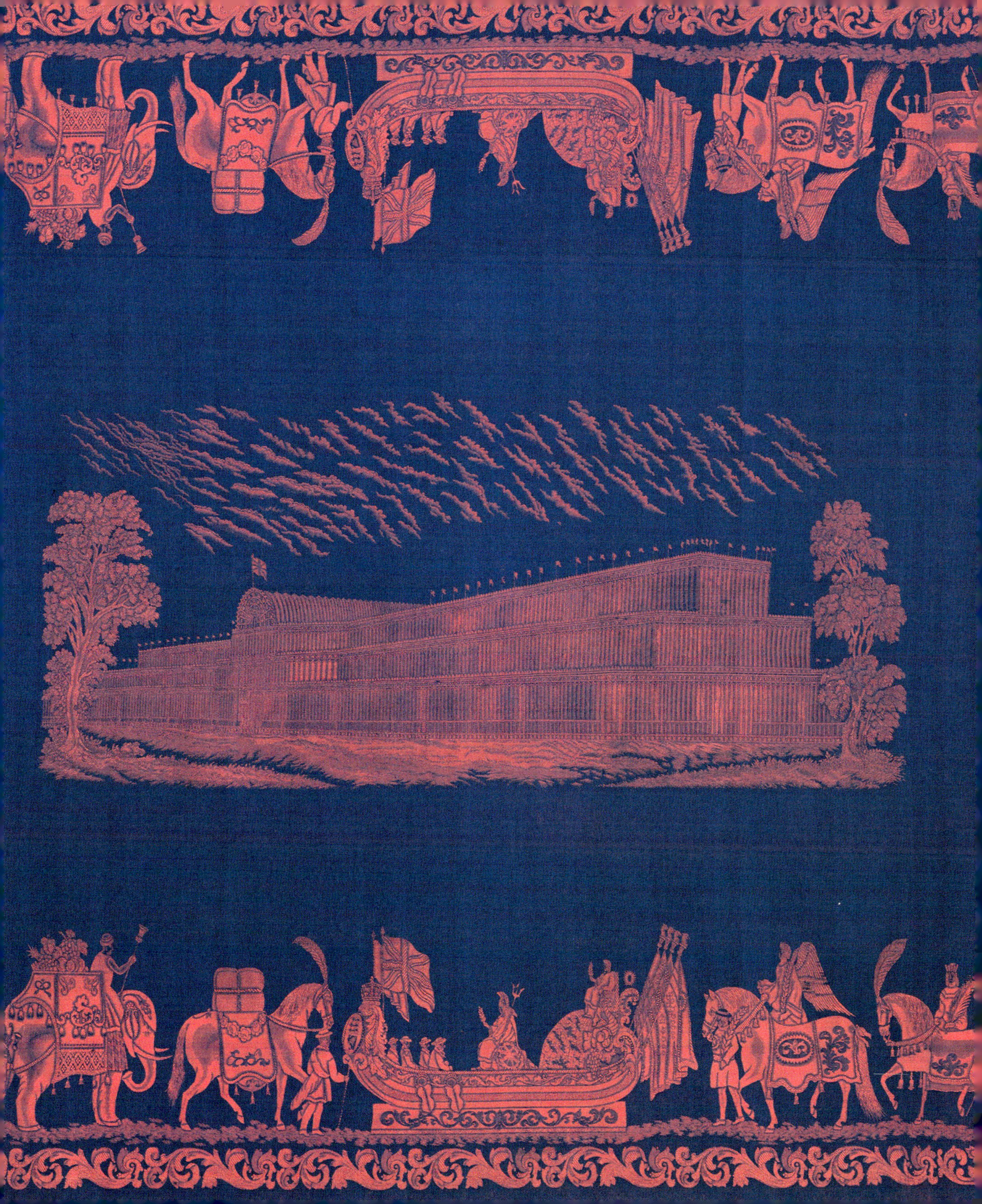

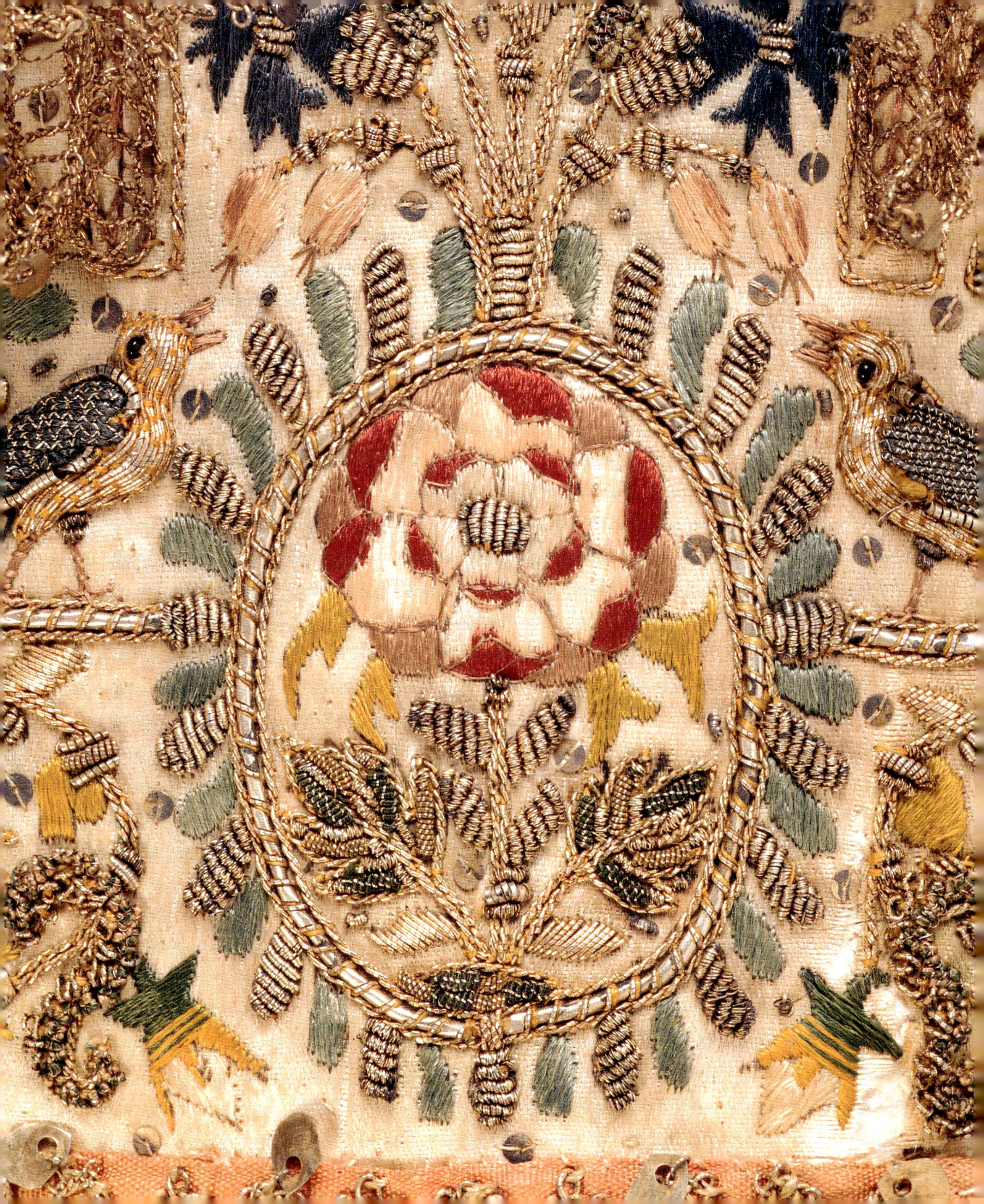

WEEK 42	October

Holiday, Canada (Thanksgiving Day)
Holiday, USA (Columbus Day)

Monday 11

Tuesday 12

Wednesday 13

Thursday 14

New Moon

Friday 15

First Day of Ramadân (subject to sighting of the moon)

Saturday 16

Sunday 17

Cream leather glove (detail), *with satin gauntlet embroidered with silk and metal thread and spangles. Trimmed with silk ribbon and silver-gilt bobbin lace. English, 1600–1625.*

October

WEEK 43

18 Monday

19 Tuesday

20 Wednesday

First Quarter

21 Thursday

22 Friday

23 Saturday

24 Sunday

United Nations Day

Curtain from a set of bed hangings (detail), embroidered in crewel on a cotton and linen ground. English, 1695–1720.

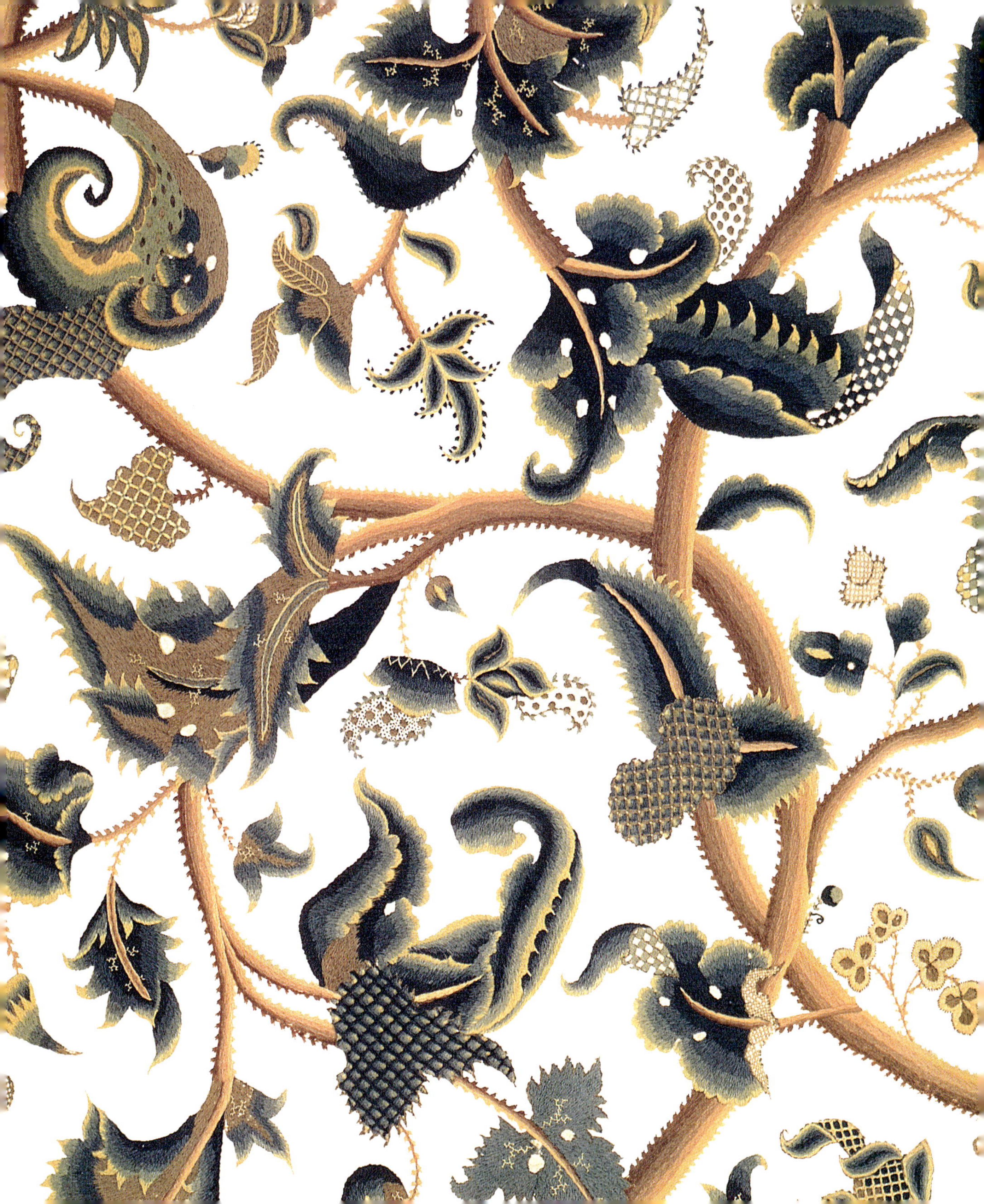

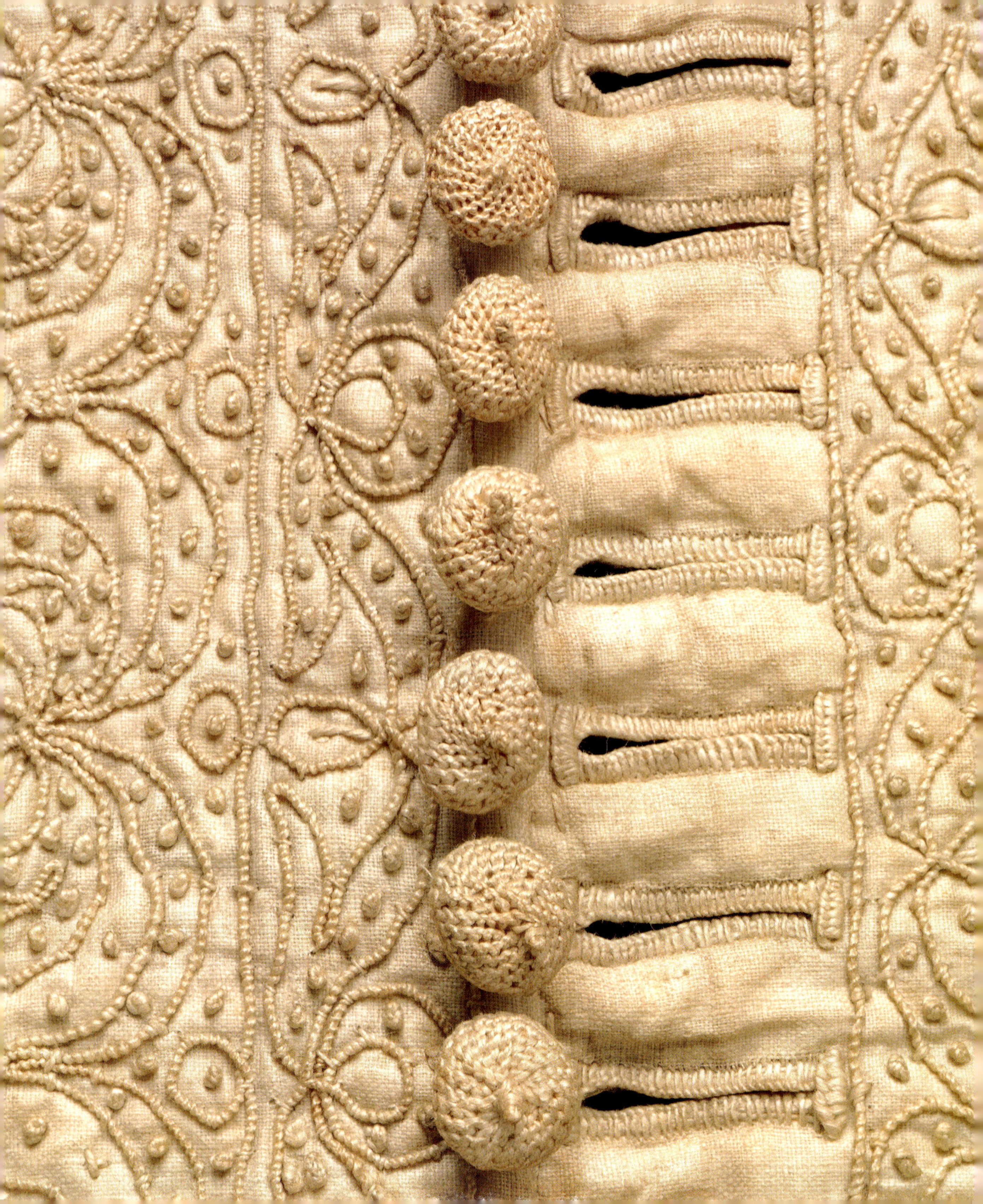

WEEK 44

October

Monday 25

Holiday, Republic of Ireland
Holiday, New Zealand (Labour Day)

Tuesday 26

Wednesday 27

Thursday 28

Full Moon

Friday 29

Saturday 30

Sunday 31

Hallowe'en
British Summer Time ends

A man's doublet (detail), *glazed bleached linen embroidered in linen thread. English, 1635–1640.*

November

WEEK 45

1 Monday

All Saints' Day

2 Tuesday

3 Wednesday

4 Thursday

5 Friday

Last Quarter
Guy Fawkes' Day

6 Saturday

7 Sunday

A sack-back gown (detail), *made from silk woven in Spitalfields, London. English, about 1755–1760.*

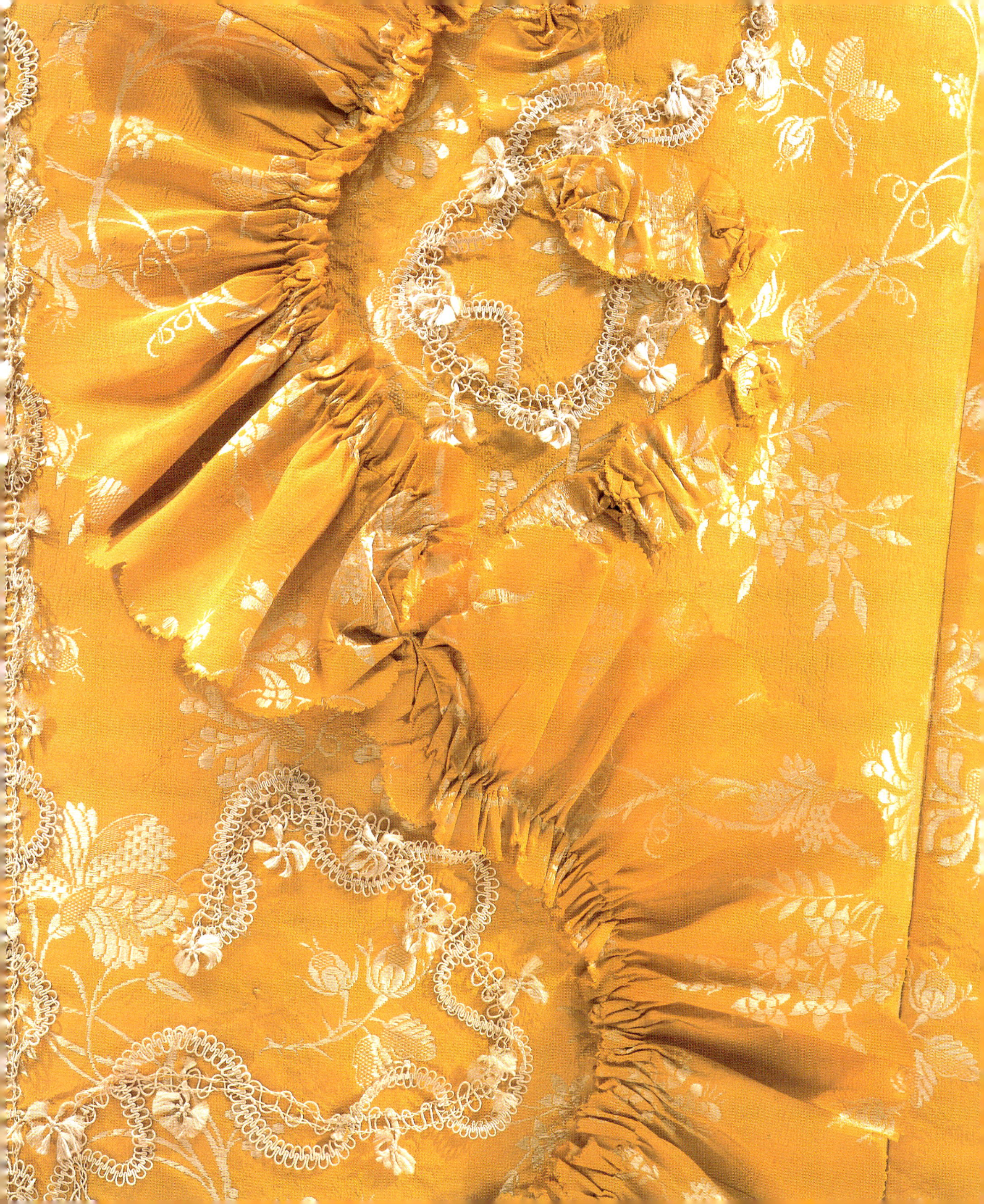

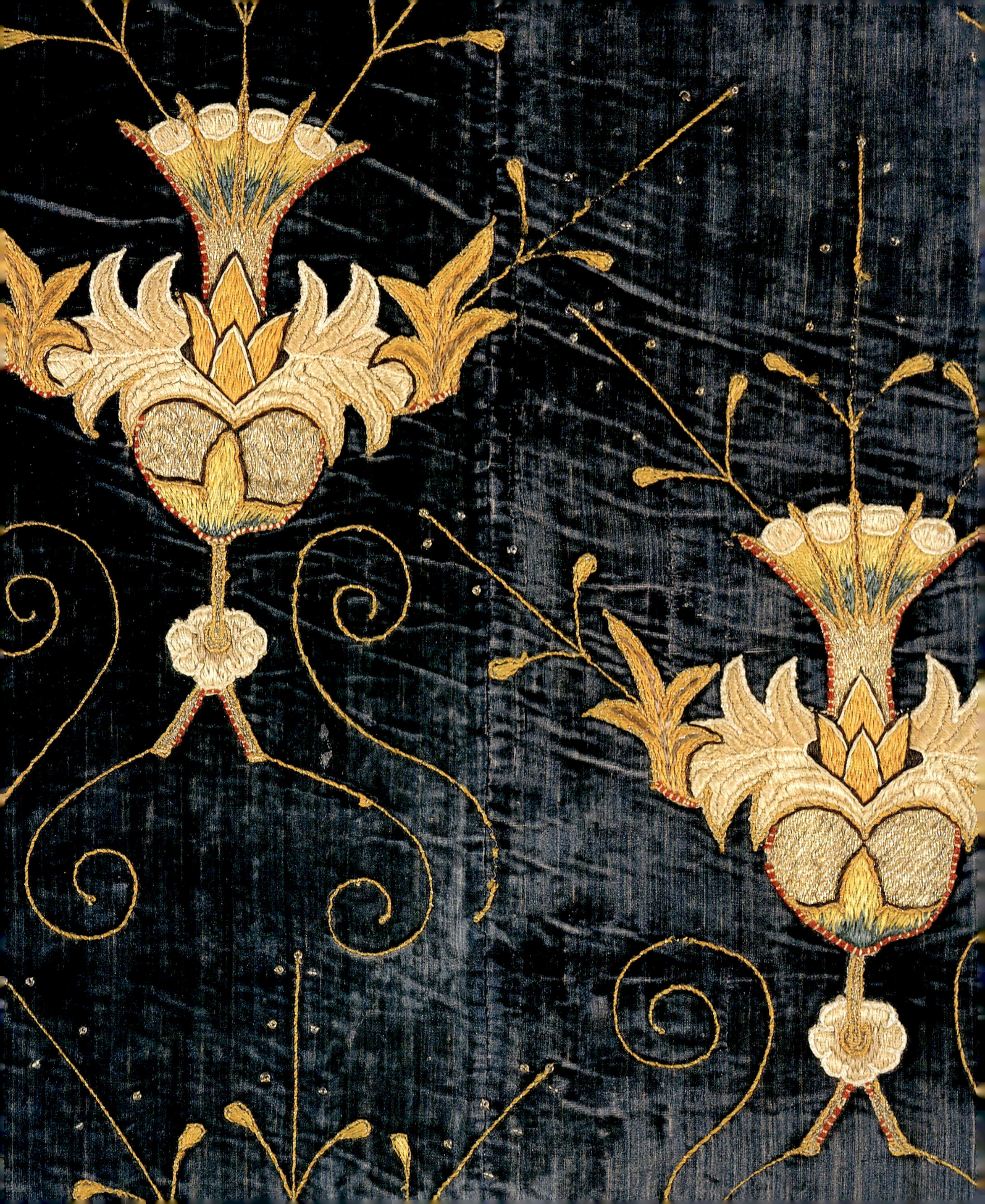

WEEK 46

November

Monday 8

Tuesday 9

Wednesday 10

Thursday 11

Holiday, Canada (Remembrance Day)
Holiday, USA (Veterans' Day)

Friday 12

New Moon

Saturday 13

Sunday 14

Remembrance Sunday, UK

Fragment of an altar frontal. Silk velvet, with linen applied and embroidered in silver-gilt and silk threads in couched work and split stitch. Velvet probably from Italy; embroidered and made up in England, 1470–1500

November

WEEK 47

15 Monday

16 Tuesday

17 Wednesday

18 Thursday

19 Friday

First Quarter

20 Saturday

21 Sunday

Mantua or court dress (detail). Silk embroidered with coloured silk and silver thread. English, 1740–1745.

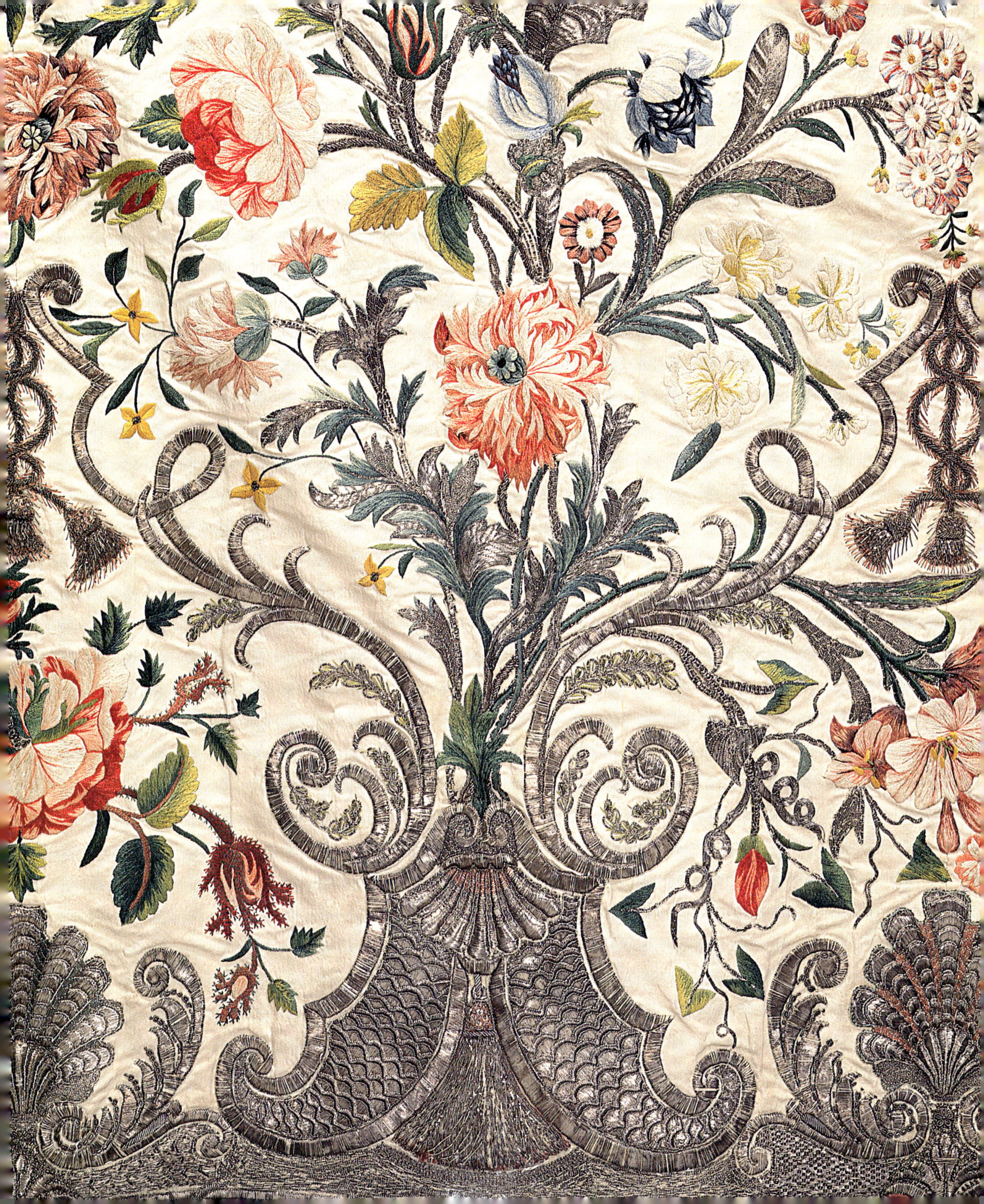

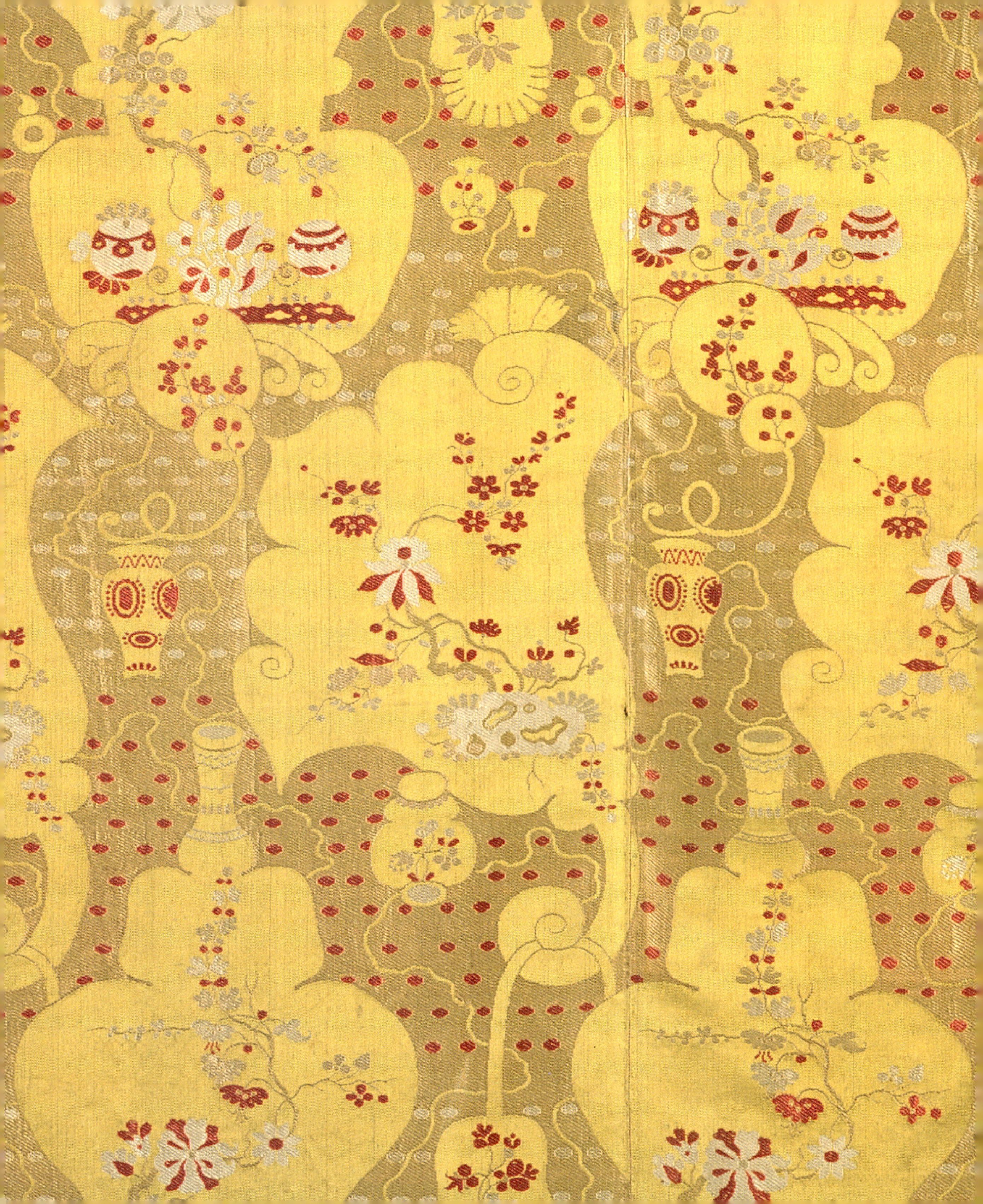

WEEK 48

November

Monday 22

Tuesday 23

Wednesday 24

Thursday 25

Holiday, USA (Thanksgiving Day)

Friday 26

Full Moon

Saturday 27

Sunday 28

Advent Sunday

Brocaded satin dress fabric, woven in Spitalfields, London. English, about 1709.

November/December

WEEK 49

29 Monday

30 Tuesday

1 Wednesday

St Andrew's Day

2 Thursday

3 Friday

4 Saturday

5 Sunday

Last Quarter

Woven woollen double cloth curtain, designed by C.F.A. Voysey and manufactured by Alexander Moreton & Co. English, 1896–1900.

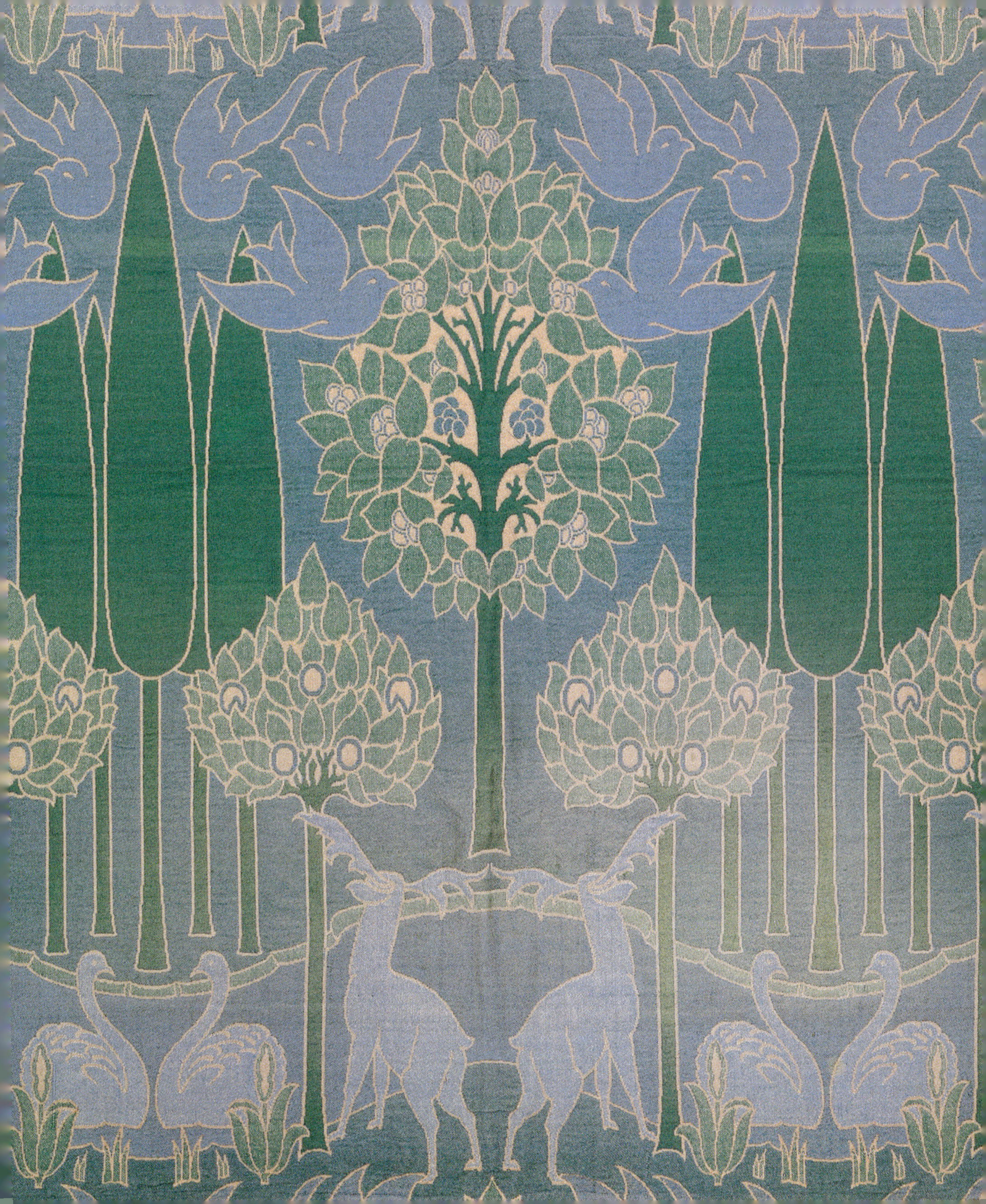

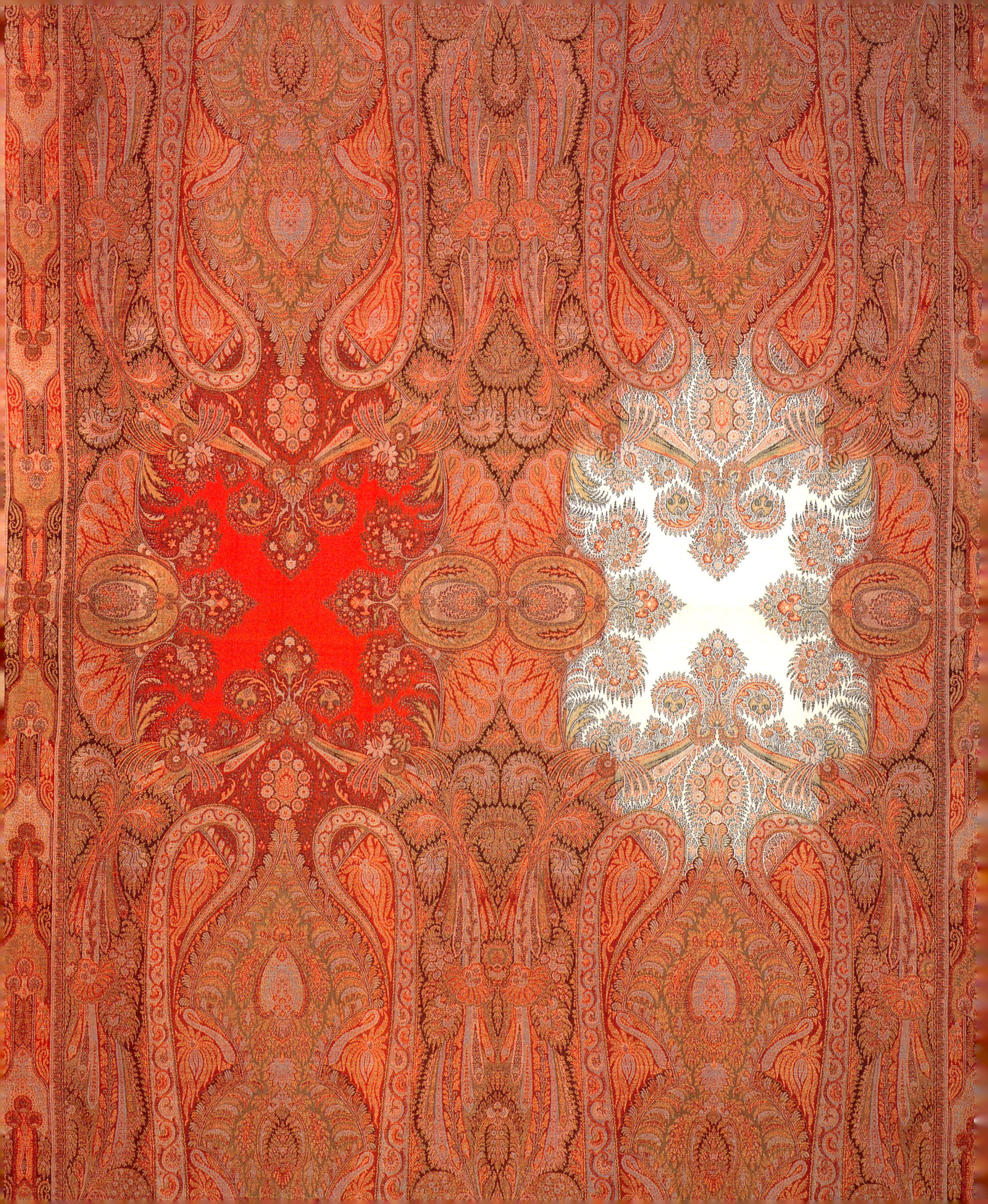

WEEK 50

December

Monday 6

Tuesday 7

Wednesday 8

Jewish Festival of Chanukah, First Day

Thursday 9

Friday 10

Saturday 11

Sunday 12

New Moon

'Paisley' shawl, woven in wool on a jacquard loom.
Probably made in Paisley. British, 1851–1855.

December

WEEK 51

13 Monday

14 Tuesday

15 Wednesday

16 Thursday

17 Friday

18 Saturday

First Quarter

19 Sunday

Seat cover for a settee, embroidered on canvas in wool and silk. English, 1730–1740.

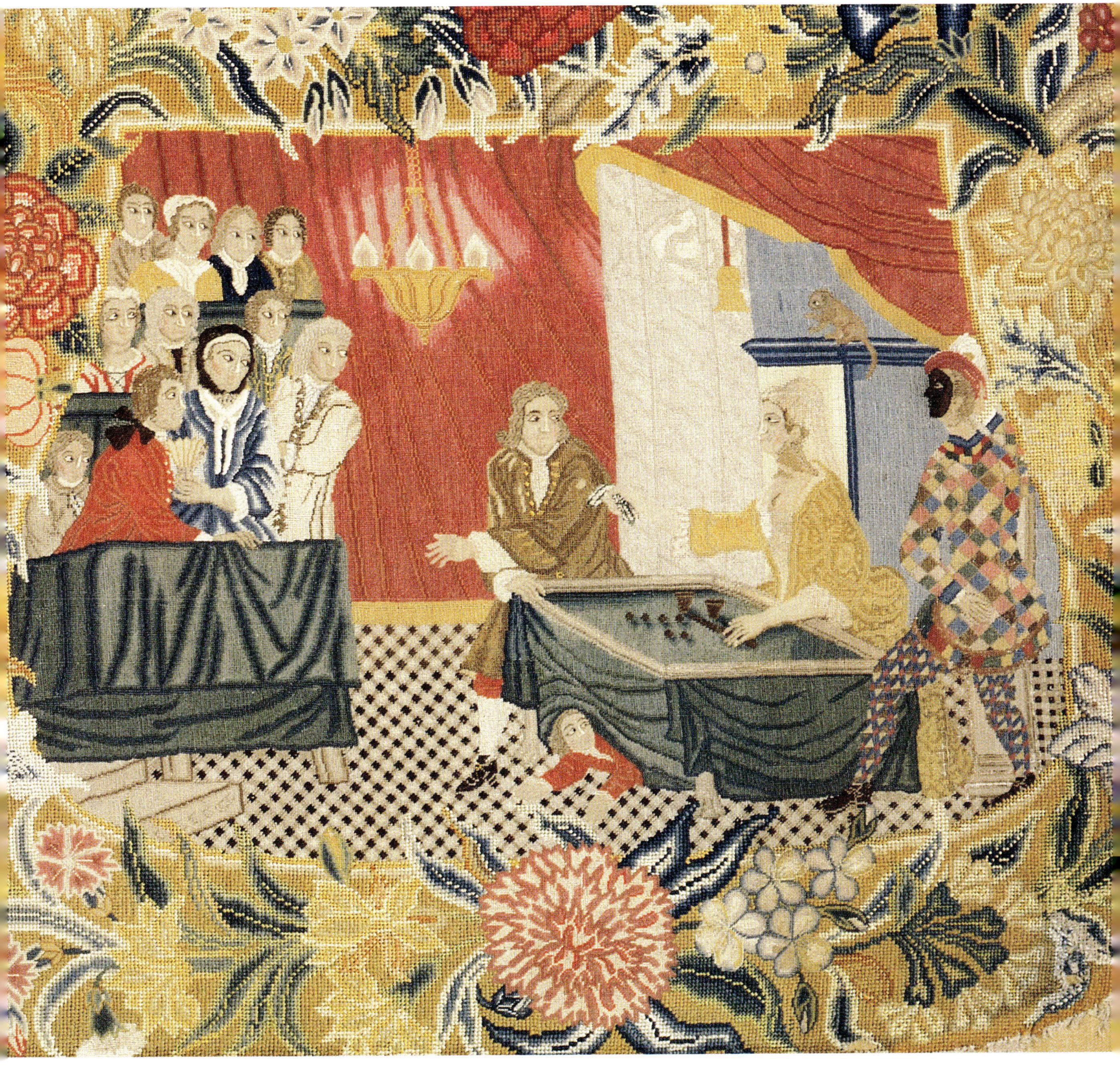

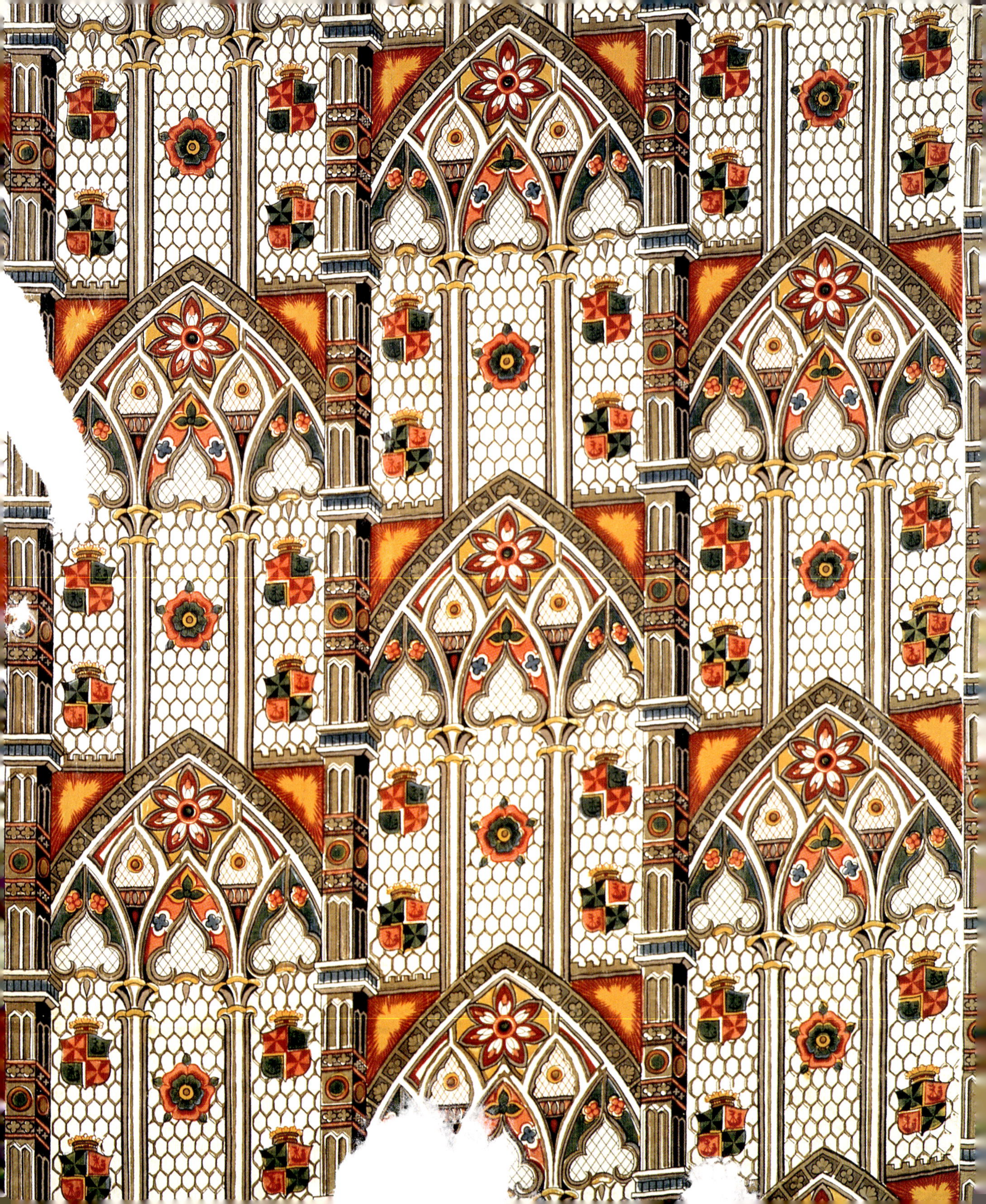

WEEK 52

December

Monday 20

Tuesday 21

Winter Solstice

Wednesday 22

Thursday 23

Friday 24

Christmas Eve
Holiday, USA (Christmas Day observed)

Saturday 25

Christmas Day

Sunday 26

Full Moon
Boxing Day (St Stephen's Day)

Printed cotton furnishing fabric, depicting
Gothic windows. English, about 1830.

December/January

WEEK 53

27 Monday

Holiday UK, Republic of Ireland, Canada, Australia and New Zealand

28 Tuesday

Holiday, UK, Republic of Ireland, Canada, Australia and New Zealand

29 Wednesday

30 Thursday

31 Friday

New Year's Eve
Holiday, USA (New Year's Day observed)

1 Saturday

New Year's Day

2 Sunday

Card N.º 8.

Page of a textile sample book for the Spanish and Portuguese markets, produced for John Kelly, a Norwich worsted manufacturer. Worsted wool samples mounted on paper. English, 1763.

66

Fine Martiniques, 18 In.: 32 yds.
From N.º 63 to N.º 67.

74.
75.
76.
77.
78.
79.
80.
81.
82.
83.
Card.
Nº 8.

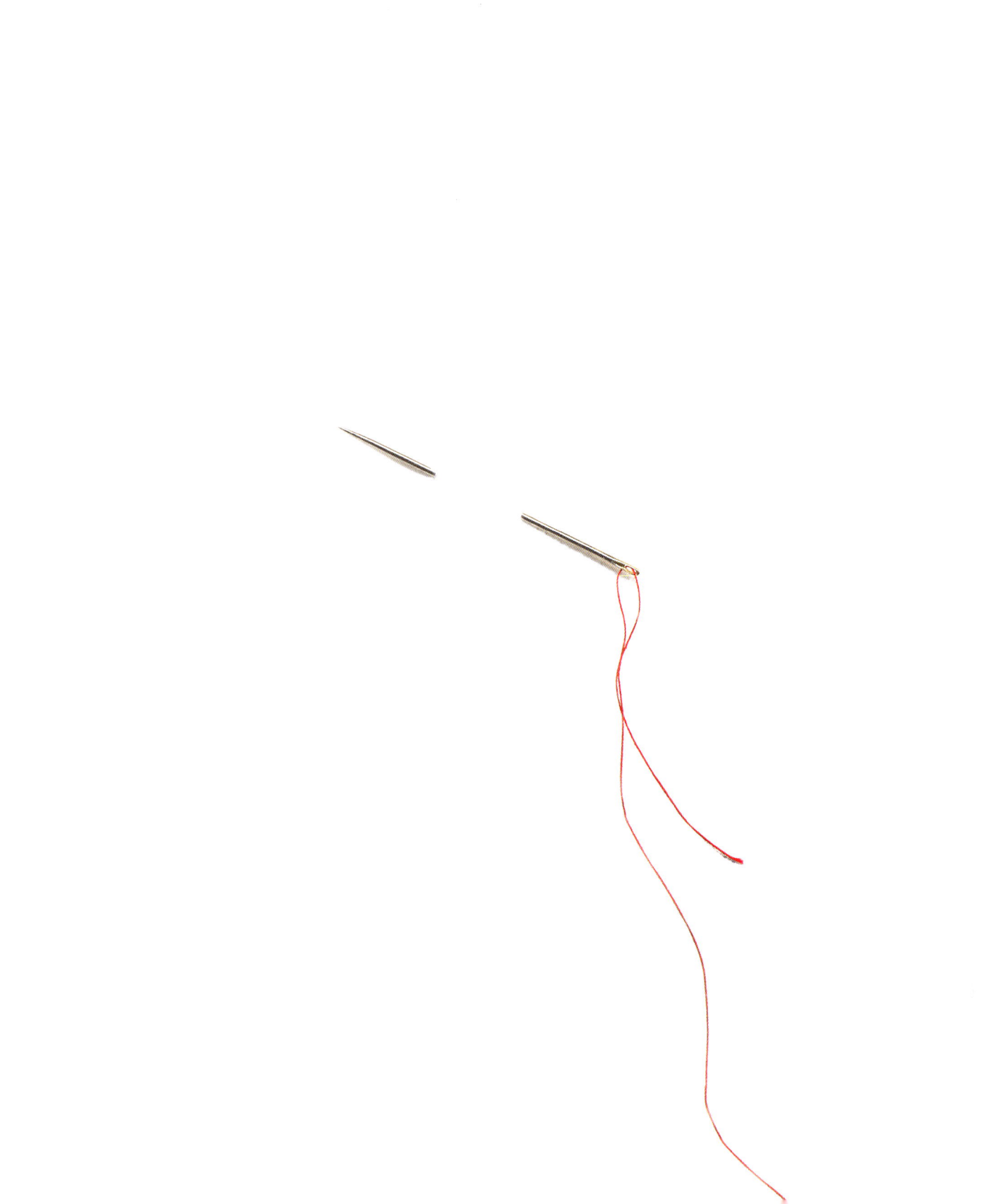